WORLD
HISTORY SERIES ■ ■ ■

The Chinese Cultural Revolution

Titles in the World History Series

WORLD HISTORY SERIES ■ ■ ■

The Chinese Cultural Revolution

by
David Pietrusza

Lucent Books, P.O. Box 289011, San Diego, CA 92198-9011

Library of Congress Cataloging-in-Publication Data

Pietrusza, David, 1949–
    The Chinese Cultural Revolution / by David Pietrusza.
        p. cm.—(World history series)
    Includes bibliographical references and index.
    Summary: Describes the events surrounding the Maoist
revolution in China.
    ISBN 1-56006-305-X
    1. China—History—Cultural Revolution, 1966–1969—
Juvenile literature.   2. China—Politics and government—
1949–1976—Juvenile literature.   [1. China—History—
Cultural Revolution, 1966–1969.   2. China—History—
1949–1976.   I.Title.   II. Series.
DS778.7.P54   1997
951.05'6—dc20   96-16442
                                                       CIP
                                                        AC

Copyright 1997 by Lucent Books, Inc., P.O. Box 289011,
San Diego, California 92198-9011

Printed in the U.S.A.

Contents

Foreword

Each year on the first day of school, nearly every history teacher faces the task of explaining why his or her students should study history. One logical answer to this question is that exploring what happened in our past explains how the things we often take for granted—our customs, ideas, and institutions—came to be. As statesman and historian Winston Churchill put it, "Every nation or group of nations has its own tale to tell. Knowledge of the trials and struggles is necessary to all who would comprehend the problems, perils, challenges, and opportunities which confront us today." Thus, a study of history puts modern ideas and institutions in perspective. For example, though the founders of the United States were talented and creative thinkers, they clearly did not invent the concept of democracy. Instead, they adapted some democratic ideas that had originated in ancient Greece and with which the Romans, the British, and others had experimented. An exploration of these cultures, then, reveals their very real connection to us through institutions that continue to shape our daily lives.

Another reason often given for studying history is the idea that lessons exist in the past from which contemporary societies can benefit and learn. This idea, although controversial, has always been an intriguing one for historians. Those that agree that society can benefit from the past often quote philosopher George Santayana's famous statement, "Those who cannot remember the past are condemned to repeat it." Historians who ascribe to Santayana's philosophy believe that, for example, studying the events that led up to the major world wars or other significant historical events would allow society to chart a different and more favorable course in the future.

Just as difficult as convincing students to realize the importance of studying history is the search for useful and interesting supplementary materials that present historical events in a context that can be easily understood. The volumes in Lucent Books' World History Series attempt to present a broad, balanced, and penetrating view of the march of history. Ancient Egypt's important wars and rulers, for example, are presented against the rich and colorful backdrop of Egyptian religious, social, and cultural developments. The series engages the reader by enhancing historical events with these cultural contexts. For example, in *Ancient Greece*, the text covers the role of women in that society. Slavery is discussed in *The Roman Empire*, as well as how slaves earned their freedom. The numerous and varied aspects of everyday life in these and other societies are explored in each volume of the series. Additionally, the series covers the major political, cultural, and philosophical ideas as the torch of civilization is passed from ancient Mesopotamia and Egypt, through Greece, Rome, Medieval Europe, and other world cultures, to the modern day.

The material in the series is formatted in a thorough, precise, and organized manner. Each volume offers the reader a comprehensive and clearly written overview of an important historical event or period. The topic under discussion is placed in a broad historical context. For example, *The Italian Renaissance* begins with a discussion of the High Middle Ages and the loss of central control that allowed certain Italian cities to develop artistically. The book ends by looking forward to the Reformation and interpreting the societal changes that grew out of the Renaissance. Thus, students are not only involved in an historical era, but also enveloped by the events leading up to that era and the events following it.

One important and unique feature in the World History Series is the primary and secondary source quotations that richly supplement each volume. These quotes are useful in a number of ways. First, they allow students access to sources they would not normally be exposed to because of the difficulty and obscurity of the original source. The quotations range from interesting anecdotes to farsighted cultural perspectives and are drawn from historical witnesses both past and present. Second, the quotes demonstrate how and where historians themselves derive their information on the past as they strive to reach a consensus on historical events. Lastly, all of the quotes are footnoted, familiarizing students with the citation process and allowing them to verify quotes and/or look up the original source if the quote piques their interest.

Finally, the books in the World History Series provide a detailed launching point for further research. Each book contains a bibliography specifically geared toward student research. A second, annotated bibliography introduces students to all the sources the author consulted when compiling the book. A chronology of important dates gives students an overview, at a glance, of the topic covered. Where applicable, a glossary of terms is included.

In short, the series is designed not only to acquaint readers with the basics of history, but also to make them aware that their lives are a part of an ongoing human saga. Perhaps they will then come to the same realization as famed historian Arnold Toynbee. In his monumental work, *A Study of History*, he wrote about becoming aware of history flowing through him in a mighty current, and of his own life "welling like a wave in the flow of this vast tide."

Important Dates in the History of the Chinese Cultural Revolution

1911	1921	1934–35	1938	1949	1958	1959	1965	1966	1967	1968

1911
Qing dynasty, China's imperial family, overthrown (October 10).

1921
Mao helps found the Chinese Communist Party (July 21).

1934–35
The Long March, Mao's epic retreat from KMT armies, takes place.

1938
Mao marries Jiang Qing.

1949
Mao leads Communist takeover of Chinese mainland; renames the country People's Republic of China.

1958
Mao announces the Great Leap Forward (May 5).

1959
Mao ends the Great Leap Forward. Liu Shaoqi replaces Mao as state president. Lin Biao becomes defense minister.

1965
Wu Han's play *Hai Rui Dismissed from Office* is criticized in the press (November 10), starting the Cultural Revolution. Luo Ruiqing placed under house arrest (December 15).

1966
Lin Biao appoints Jiang Qing as cultural advisor to the armed forces. PLA occupies Beijing (March). Peng Zhen purged (May 16). Nie Yuanzi posts her first big-character poster (May 25). First Red Guard units appear in China's universities (May 29). Lin Biao named second ranking party member. Liu Shaoqi demoted (August).

1967
Radicals seize the Foreign Ministry (January 18). Deng Xiaoping purged as general secretary. Local PLA mutinies in Wuhan (June).

1968
Liu Shaoqi expelled from the CCP (October 13).

1969

Lin Biao named Mao's successor at Ninth Party Congress (April 14).

1971

Lin Biao dies (September 12).

1975

Deng Xiaoping becomes vice-chairman of the CCP (January). Kang Sheng dies (December 16).

1976

Mao Zedong dies (September 9). Hua Guofeng becomes CCP first secretary. Gang of Four arrested (October 6).

1977

Deng Xiaoping is restored to all his party posts (July).

1978

Democracy Movement begins (November).

1980

Hua Guofeng resigns as premier. Zhao Ziyang becomes premier (September).

1981

Hua Guofeng resigns as CCP chairman.

1982

Deng becomes chairman of the party's Central Advisory Commission. Hu Yaobang becomes CCP general secretary.

1987

Zhao Ziyang replaces Hu Yaobang as general secretary (January 16).

1989

Hu Yaobang dies (April 15). Tiananmen Square demonstration crushed (June 4). Jiang Zemin replaces Zhao Ziyang as general secretary.

1993

Li Ping reelected as premier. Jiang Zemin elected state president.

The Quest for a More Prosperous Nation

In the 1960s Mao Zedong's violent Cultural Revolution set the People's Republic of China (PRC) on a decade-long course of unprecedented and savage public turmoil. As Mao Zedong fought to regain unlimited power to implement a radical version of socialist revolution, millions would die; millions more would be imprisoned or persecuted before China could return to relative peacefulness.

To understand the Cultural Revolution, however, it is necessary to understand nearly a century of Chinese history and thousands of years of Chinese culture.

Once China had been the world's most advanced nation. While much of Europe and the Americas languished in barbarism, during the Han dynasty (202 B.C.–A.D. 220) the Chinese developed such innovations as paper, and even the first seismograph. Chinese emperors ruled over a vast area, and Chinese culture was far more sophisticated than that of European nations. The situation changed after the Industrial Revolution greatly strengthened Europe's economies. China, however, not only did not move forward; it fell far behind the West. By the nineteenth century China had tumbled into a period of serious weakness and decay.

Chinese peasants and workers suffered from tremendous poverty and oppression. Landowners and business owners grew rich while millions of ordinary Chinese endured lives of grueling poverty. In the nineteenth century great famines and floods swept over China and made already difficult conditions even harsher.

Aggressive Western nations such as Britain and France took full advantage of China's problems, often seizing parts of China's territory and controlling portions of China they did not seize. Such behavior created a bitter sense of nationalism among the Chinese people, who longed to throw off foreign domination.

The Promises of Communism

In 1911 the old, corrupt, ineffectual Chinese imperial government collapsed. The Chinese saw the ideals of socialism and communism as a way to regain control of their nation and to dramatically improve the lives of ordinary Chinese men and women. Communism promised to give farmers land to till and to provide better conditions for workers in China's small

At the end of the bitter Chinese civil war in 1949, Shanghai residents celebrate the Communist victory by carrying a poster of Mao through the streets.

but growing industries. From 1921, Mao Zedong's Chinese Communist Party pledged to reverse China's decline, to free it from foreign domination, and to rid its government of corruption. A bitter civil war resulted as the Communists fought Chinese Nationalists for power. When that war ended in 1949, Mao and his fellow Communist Party members ruled the entire Chinese mainland. For a while many Chinese thought the Communists had succeeded in creating an independent, stable, and more prosperous nation.

By the early 1960s, the People's Republic had been in power for more than a decade. A more practical and less revolutionary way of thinking was replacing the enthusiastic socialism of the early years of Communist rule. Communizing, (or state control) of many of China's institutions may have been good Maoist ideology, but the idea didn't always work in practice. Many of China's leaders no longer believed that Mao's brand of radical socialism was the answer to China's problems, particularly after some of his ideas, such as the Great Leap Forward, not only failed to improve China's economy but also created chaos and even horrible famines. Moderate officials such as China's president Liu Shaoqi and his extremely able assistant Deng Xiaoping rejected Mao's radical vision and began to implement their own more pragmatic ideas.

Starting in 1965 a titanic power struggle began in China. It lasted for nearly a decade, and in 1966 received an official name from China's leadership: The Cultural Revolution. Through the Cultural Revolution Mao attempted to mobilize the masses, the peasants, the workers, and particularly university and high school students against his enemies in the Communist Party and the state bureaucracy. Mao's opponents, including Liu Shaoqi, Deng Xiaoping and their followers, would be exposed and routed out, no matter how influential or high up they were.

The Cultural Revolution promised the Chinese people not only that the exploitation of workers and peasants by landlords and capitalists would cease but also that the revolution would go forward at breakneck speed. Workers, peasants, and intellectuals would achieve equality within society that they had never known in pre-Communist China or even under the Communists. A classless society would finally be created. People still had great faith in Mao and believed that these great changes could finally occur.

Fanatical Followers

The Cultural Revolution's goals, however, were far loftier than its actions. In its name vicious Maoists publicly taunted

Young Maoist guardsmen wave Mao's little red book in 1966, demonstrating the almost cultish nature of Mao's popularity among the people.

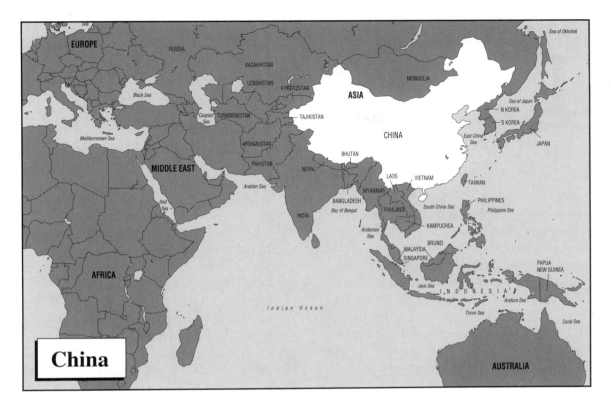

China

hundreds of thousands of high-ranking officials and ordinary persons and forced them to abjectly confess their supposed crimes. Many of Mao's opponents were beaten and later died from harsh treatment. Chanting mobs of Red Guards, Mao's most fanatical young followers ran through China's streets, frantically waving copies of Mao's collected writings and brutally humiliating their political and personal enemies.

Once Mao had crushed his rivals and restored his own authority, however, he cannily recognized that the senseless chaos created by the Cultural Revolution and the Red Guards had to end. He used Lin Biao and the People's Liberation Army (PLA) to crush his own loyal supporters—the Red Guards. The PLA curbed the Red Guards' power and sent many of them to live in the backward Chinese countryside where they faced harsh conditions.

After Mao's death in 1976, Deng Xiaoping and others carried out further economic reforms but refused to grant long-overdue political freedoms to the Chinese people. In 1989 Deng's leadership group crushed the growing protest movement for democracy. Today, nearly five decades after Mao secured power over the Chinese people, they still await true political freedom.

The Cultural Revolution was both a mass movement of idealistic young people determined to gain true equality and a ruthless attempt by Mao and his allies to cement their personal power. It left millions of ruined lives in its wake. Millions of its victims have still not recovered from its terrible excesses.

1 The East Is Red

China's shift from feudal monarchy to modern republic was hardly smooth. The Chinese people were unaccustomed to democracy: Emperors and local landlords had long controlled national politics. On October 11, 1911, China's military overthrew the country's ancient monarchy. China became a republic, but central authority fell apart and local generals or warlords ruled the country's regions.

In Shanghai a group of educated intellectuals formed the Chinese Communist Party (CCP) in 1921. The leaders claimed to want to improve the lives of the workers and the peasants, but "there was not a worker or a peasant among them,"[1] observed Ross Terrill in *Mao: A Biography*. Among the thirteen founders of the CCP was a twenty-six-year-old primary school principal named Mao Zedong.

Mao

Mao Zedong came from an extremely humble background. Born in 1893 to a peasant family in Hunan province, he briefly served in the army that helped overthrow the last Chinese imperial dynasty. Mao later graduated from the Hunan First Normal School, a teacher's college, and worked for a short time as a library assistant at Beijing University. By 1919 he was solidly involved in radical politics and had returned home to Hunan where he worked to achieve his political goal of Communist revolution.

Despite being one of the CCP's founders, Mao was nonetheless not very influential in it. Real power in the party rested in leaders based in Shanghai and in the CCP's Soviet patrons who supplied cash to the party and in return felt free to issue orders to CCP officials.

Mao also had some ideas that got him into trouble with the party leaders. Mao was actively disliked by Soviet leader Joseph Stalin, for example. Mao once recalled that Stalin called him "a turnip . . . red [Communist] on the outside but white [reactionary] on the inside."[2] Mao believed that the peasants, who were the vast bulk of China's population, were far more important to communism's victory than was China's still small but growing urban working class. In September 1926 Mao wrote a paper called "the National Revolution and the Peasant Movement," in which he contended that "the peasant question is the central question in the national revolution."[3] To many Marxist party members Mao's doctrine was heresy. They thought it was the working class who should lead the revolution.

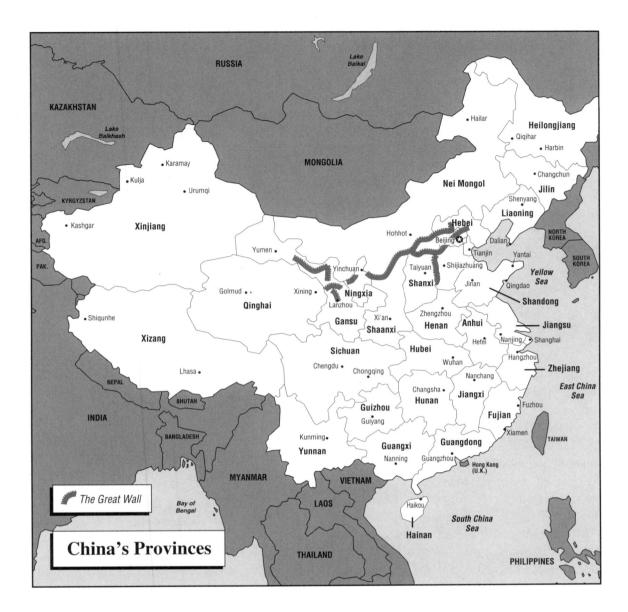

The Great Wall

China's Provinces

Power Struggle

When Mao helped found the Chinese Communist Party, it was formally part of the Kuomintang (KMT), a party founded in 1911 to eliminate foreign influences in China and led for many years by Chiang Kai-shek, a young military commander.

The KMT and the CCP soon parted ways. As the Chinese Communist Party grew so did its ambitions—much to the alarm of both the KMT and Moscow. The KMT was afraid that the CCP might try to gain control of the Chinese territory it had wrested away from the warlords. The KMT now prepared to crush the Chinese Communist Party.

Even as a young man Mao was ambitious, finding ways to form a rival organization to challenge the reigning KMT.

In 1927 the Chinese Communist Party seized control of Shanghai, China's largest and most cosmopolitan city. "The Communist leaders," noted John Byron and Robert Pack in *The Claws of the Dragon*, "were convinced that victory over the warlord administration in Shanghai was the beginning of a revolutionary upsurge that would bring about a new social order."[4] Chiang feared exactly the same thing—and also feared the Soviets. His suspicions were not unreasonable. Soviet leader Joseph Stalin had privately said of Chiang, "We shall squeeze him like a lemon and then get rid of him."[5] With the help of Shanghai's gangster elements, known as the Green Gang, the anti-Communist Chiang crushed the Shanghai CCP's "citizens' government." This event was the be-

ginning of a violent systematic purge of Communists from the KMT.

Mao's Climb to Power

For the next several years, the Kuomintang-controlled Chinese central government kept Mao and China's Communists on the defensive. KMT secret police infiltrated the CCP underground and arrested numerous party leaders. An atmosphere of secretiveness, endless plotting, intrigue, and outright paranoia was rampant among CCP leadership. Such attitudes would linger far after Chinese Communists triumphed over Chiang Kai-shek in 1949, particularly in regard to those once arrested and released by the KMT.

As the KMT's secret police routed out Communists in Shanghai and other major cities, the influence of rural CCP leaders such as Mao Zedong grew.

"A Revolution Is Not a Dinner Party"

Mao believed that outright force against the KMT and the Chinese government was the only way to achieve victory. In 1927 he wrote:

> A revolution is not a dinner party, or writing an essay, or painting a picture, or doing embroidery; it cannot be so refined, so leisurely and gentle, so temperate, kind, courteous, restrained, and magnanimous. A revolution is an insurrection, an act of violence by which one class overthrows another.[6]

With the CCP's base in the cities greatly weakened, Mao and others not only recruited supporters in the countryside but also formed a small, functional peasant army dedicated to battling the KMT and bringing about a Communist revolution.

Mao also wooed many middle-class professionals by appealing to their sense of patriotism and convinced them that the CCP was their best hope of freeing China from foreign domination. Mao also increased popular support by running his army in an open and fair way—a very rare practice among China's often dictatorial generals. "Each man," summed up Ross Terrill in *Mao: A Biography*, "came to feel part of a shared crusade."[7]

Still Mao's achievements didn't impress the CCP's Moscow-appointed leadership. In March 1928 the leaders harshly rebuked Mao for his ideas of a peasant-based revolution, but Mao nevertheless managed to survive and eventually increase his strength.

The Long March

In 1934 KMT troops went on the offensive against Mao's forces, which were then in South China, surrounding his army and hoping to crush the Communists once and for all. Mao resolved to regroup in a remote area to the north. He led a hundred thousand supporters (eighty-five thousand troops and fifteen thousand auxiliary personnel) away from the KMT's encircling armies. Mao's escape from KMT armies, the so-called Long March, became one of the great journeys of modern times.

The Long March lasted from October 1934 to October 1935 as Mao zigged and zagged across China to evade KMT troops. Finally Mao's forces felt safe enough to regroup at Ya'an in remote northern Shaanxi province. His beleaguered army had traveled six thousand miles (ten thousand kilometers), crossed eleven provinces and eighteen mountain ranges, and forded twenty-four rivers. Only 10 percent of those he started with at Jiangsi a year before survived the Long March. The rest either deserted or perished from KMT attacks, exhaustion, sickness, or starvation.

Nevertheless, the Long March was a tremendous success for Mao. His survival against enormous odds made him a military legend, especially among the rural peasants. To encourage their support, Mao's troops would continually tell the peasants that they would receive land if the CCP gained power.

Before beginning the Long March, Mao was just one of several influential CCP leaders. At Ya'an Mao finally emerged as the unchallenged ruler of Chinese communism. No CCP leader based in far-off Shanghai would challenge his leadership; no one from Moscow would issue him orders. Mao had established an independent power base that no one could influence.

Like the KMT, Mao developed his own way of dealing with dissenters as well as with suspected KMT or Japanese agents. In Ya'an the CCP's social affairs department, under the brilliant but brutal Kang Sheng, used torture to force confessions and persecute rivals. In February 1942 the party's Rectification movement, again under Kang Sheng's direction, employed torture and imprisonment to bring into line anyone who questioned Mao's status. Mao had become a dictator of the Chinese Communist Party.

The Sino-Japanese War

As Mao settled into his new headquarters in Ya'an, a new threat confronted China. Starting in 1931, the Japanese began seizing China's northern region, Manchuria. By 1932 they completely controlled the area, creating a puppet state called Manchukuo. They were, however, not content with just Manchuria. Soon they marched southward, encroaching further on Chinese territory. By July 1937 the Japanese empire and the KMT forces controlling the Republic of China were engaged in open warfare.

Mao was already determined to resist the Japanese and decided to unite with the KMT to achieve his goal. The Japanese invasion also meant that China could no longer afford the luxury of its internal battle between Chiang's often corrupt Nationalists and Mao's Communists. In 1937 the two warring factions announced a cease-fire and declared that they would cooperate in a united front against their common Japanese enemy.

The KMT Collapses

The fight against the Japanese harmed the Nationalists more than it did the Communists, because the Japanese seized far more KMT territory, along China's seacoast, than CCP territory, deep in China's interior. In December 1941 Britain and the United States declared war against Japan. Their efforts helped ensure Japan's defeat in 1945 and its withdrawal from Chinese territory.

With Japan subdued, the reason for KMT-CCP cooperation vanished, and in March 1946 open hostilities resumed. Mao's forces were still significantly inferior to Chiang's. In 1945, when World War II concluded, the Nationalists had 3.7 million soldiers under arms; Mao's Red Army numbered 320,000, of whom only 166,000 were armed. Even Soviet dictator Joseph Stalin urged Mao to dissolve his army and join Chiang's government. Mao refused.

During the war against Japan, the CCP had grown dramatically, and with war's end, the KMT-controlled Republic of China was racked by hyperinflation. At one point it took ninety-three thousand Chinese dollars to obtain one U.S. dollar. Riots and work stoppages plagued the major cities. The KMT paid its soldiers in worthless paper money, and to make ends meet they were soon selling their weapons—to Mao's soldiers. Mao was also aided by his not-always-friendly allies, the Soviets. The 1945 Yalta agreement between the USSR, the United States, and the United Kingdom allowed the Soviet Union to occupy Manchuria after Japan surrendered. Before leaving Manchuria, the Soviet army transferred many captured Japanese arms to Mao's military. In June 1948 KMT forces had shrunk to just 1.5 million soldiers, while Mao's Red Army had grown to that same strength and was armed with one million rifles.

The Red Army under such generals as Lin Biao waged a seemingly unstoppable campaign against Chiang, using not only military strategies but also highly sophisticated political ones. On seizing an area, Lin immediately distributed rich land-

The Long March

Legend:
- Elevation over 6000'
- The Long March

lords' land to poor sharecroppers, thus building up a base of support. He let KMT commanders surrender under generous terms and often allowed them to become officers in the Red Army. He even used captured Japanese artillery experts to train Red Army detachments.

By October 1949 Chiang Kai-shek had evacuated all his forces and Mao proclaimed a Communist victory by renaming the mainland the People's Republic of China. He now controlled China.

Immediately after seizing power, the Communists sent twenty million people—

convicted of being landlords, rich peasants, counterrevolutionaries, or bad elements—to prisons and labor camps. The Communists were settling scores against those who had supported the KMT, against those who had wealthy or middle-class backgrounds, and against those with Western educations or connections.

Mao's government admitted to executing nearly one million counterrevolutionaries from October 1949 to October 1950. Foreign sources estimated that the total dead through the end of 1952 was closer to two million.

Japanese troops occupy Shanghai in 1937. Mao would play a key role in helping to oust the Japanese from Chinese territory.

As part of his reforms, in early 1957 Mao startled many party members by encouraging open criticism of his regime, especially from non-Communist intellectuals. Mao told skeptics that by allowing criticism he hoped that China might avoid the difficulties that were plaguing Communist regimes in Eastern Europe, where riots threatened a number of governments.

Using a metaphor of flowers for free speech and ideas, Mao told the nation: "Letting a hundred flowers blossom and a hundred schools of thought contend is the policy for promoting progress in the arts and sciences and a flourishing socialist culture in our land."[8] By the spring of 1957 a torrent of criticism broke loose. People demanded free speech; workers wanted to organize independent unions.

Mao, however, had blatantly lied to smoke out his opponents. After just six weeks of letting a hundred flowers bloom he cracked down. Between 1957 and 1958, an additional 2.9 million party and non-party members were denounced as rightist, or insufficiently revolutionary. Mao imprisoned or sent to labor camps 550,000 people.

Land Reform

For the first few years under Mao's leadership the People's Republic achieved great economic progress. Chinese national income doubled in the 1950s. Life expectancy increased. Infant mortality dropped.

Mao's program of land reform, taking land from rich landholders and giving it to the peasants who actually worked it, helped create this relative prosperity. The peasants now had an incentive to produce more—they could keep what they earned instead of surrendering it to often greedy landlords.

Also aiding conditions in China was the simple fact that after more than three

"An Oriental Hitler"

After seizing power in 1949, Mao Zedong became the center of what Soviet premier Nikita Khrushchev called a cult of personality. Mao was held up as the model for all that was good, right, and forward thinking. Support for Mao was hardly subtle, and it is not too much of an exaggeration to say he was nearly worshiped by his subjects. The results would be calamitous for China. Author Paul Johnson wrote about Mao in Modern Times.

"In his artistic longings, in his romanticism and in his belief that will is the key not only to power but to accomplishment, Mao was an Oriental Hitler. Though the cult of Mao bore a superficial resemblance to Stalinism, it actually had a far more creative and central role in the Maoist state. Like Hitler, Mao loved politics as theatre. The decor of his regime was far more striking and original than Stalin's lacklustre imitations of Nazi pomp. He drew on and transformed the majesty of the imperial era. The crowds were trained to greet him with the ritual chant 'Boundless life to Chairman Mao.' Like the emperors, he ploughed a symbolic annual furrow, used the Imperial City for his residence and gave calligraphic instructions for monuments. But to this he added a sun-culture of his own, reflected in his hymn 'The East Is Red,' which he imposed on China as a second national anthem:

From the Red East rises the sun:
There appears in China a Mao Zedong."

Mao was able to inspire an incredible amount of loyalty among the people of China. Those who were not so loyal were kept in line through fear and intimidation.

Mao's attempt to jump-start the Chinese economy was called the Great Leap Forward, and it conspicuously failed. One of the major failures was the development of agricultural communes (below) which were inefficient and removed personal incentive. (Left) Mao, however, would not hear criticism of his efforts. Here, he inspects the communes.

decades of constant warfare the nation was finally at peace. Marauding warlords and brutal Japanese no longer ravaged the countryside. Communist and Nationalist armies no longer battled each other.

The Great Leap Forward

Mao should have been content with the early advances his regime had made, but he was not. The Chinese people were not moving fast enough or dramatically enough to satisfy his ambitious desires. On May 5, 1958, Mao instituted a radical economic program that he called the Three Red Banners, but which is known to history by the name of one of its key parts, the Great Leap Forward. Mao's program was designed to bring the People's Republic up to the economic level of the United Kingdom within fifteen years.

Mao promised to triple China's steel production from 1.7 million tons to 5.35

million tons per year and also to establish twenty-six thousand people's communes. The communes, which contained about five thousand families (up to twenty-five thousand individuals) were run by local party officials, who took control of the peasants' land and forced them into dormitories with communal kitchens and day

Because life for many had improved since the Communist Party had taken power, the People's Republic enjoyed a great amount of goodwill from the people. This popularity was invaluable when the Great Leap Forward destroyed the economy and millions died from the resulting famine. Anne F. Thurston in Enemies of the People *quoted Zhao Wenhoa, a survivor of the Great Leap Forward.*

"It was the fall of 1959, in a commune on the outskirts of Peking [Beijing]. I had been sent there to do manual labor. The press was reporting on the excellent situation, how good and glorious things were. The catchword was, 'The situation is very good and becoming better and better.' There was no food to eat in the village. The peasants were eating the leaves of trees, boiling leaves in water, mixing them with a little corn flour to make the leaves stick together, making *wotou*. But the peasants' *wotou* didn't even stick together because there wasn't enough corn flour. Actually, we intellectuals were lucky. We were eating sweet potato leaves. The best are the leaves of the sweet potato. Then the leaves of the plum. The worst are the willow leaves. The peasants were eating willow.

Most of us who had doubts remained silent. If you had doubts you were scared. You thought, 'How would I dare to doubt?' Besides, for most people, the doubt wasn't over the whole regime but over whether the party had made serious mistakes. The degree of doubt the people had shouldn't be exaggerated."

care centers. The communes stripped the peasants of such basic private property as their homes and farm animals.

To produce the promised amount of steel, Mao encouraged peasants to donate metal to construct thousands of backyard furnaces in rural China to spur China's steel production forward at a breakneck pace. So fanatical was the communal movement that even such small items as the peasants' woks, the round cooking utensils that are the center of each Chinese kitchen, were seized for steel production. Anyone who refused to contribute was punished as a subversive.

Mao believed the Great Leap Forward would allow him to surpass the Soviets economically and politically. "In the mid–twentieth century," he boasted, "the center of world revolution had shifted to China."[9]

Mao's plan was disastrous. Makeshift steel factories produced crude unusable steel. Even worse, robbing the peasants of their private property and forcing them to make steel and abandon food production ruined China's agricultural system.

A massive famine resulted, costing millions of lives, killing more than the previous two great Chinese famines—from

1869 to 1879 (once believed to be history's worst famine) and from 1926 to 1929 (which cost an estimated twenty million dead). Experts believe that between twenty-seven and thirty million Chinese died as a result of the famine created by Mao's Great Leap Forward.

Complaints about the Great Leap Forward's catastrophic failures quickly reached Mao in China's capital, Beijing, but he remained blindly optimistic. To reassure himself, in May 1959 he visited his home village of Shaoshan.

When he met with local peasants, they complained about everything—about the communal kitchens and about the steel furnaces. The Great Leap Forward simply wasn't working. Mao had no defense and told the residents, "If you can't fill your bellies at the public dining hall [communal kitchen], then it's better just to disband it. . . . And if you can't produce good steel, you might as well quit."[10]

News of Mao's words spread throughout China; communes were disbanded and steel furnaces closed. But even though Mao had been forced to retreat from his radical policies, his ego was so large that he bitterly resented any criticism, particularly when it came from those now helping him lead China's government.

A Massive Blunder

Although Mao remained popular among millions of ordinary Chinese, large elements within the PRC's top leadership no longer believed in his revolution. In November 1958, other Chinese leaders began returning the peasants' land and private property.

Members of the CCP planned to strip Mao of a significant amount—but not all—of his power. But Mao was not interested in sharing power. He wanted it all.

Chapter

2 China's Divided Leadership

Mao had lost credibility because of the Great Leap Forward, and other CCP leaders were no longer willing to let him have total control in ruling China. He retained the post of party chairman but stepped down as president of the People's Republic, that is, as head of China's government. When Liu Shaoqi replaced Mao in that post in 1959, he earned Mao's resentment. Although Mao had to share authority with Liu, he was still head of the Communist Party.

Mao's personal physician, Dr. Li Zhisui, explained Mao's resentment:

> The English rendering of *president* to denote chairman of the republic misses what was the major problem for Mao. When Liu Shaoqi took over as chairman of the republic, there were two men with the title of chairman in China, where titles and appearances are very important. This Mao would never accept.[11]

State president Liu began acting independently of Mao, often not even bothering to consult him. He reversed many of Mao's more radical policies, and in August 1961 Liu boldly stated: "We have to go into maximum retreat in both industry and agriculture. Anything that lifts the peasants' spirits is good. We can't say that

one method is best to the exclusion of all others."[12]

Mao took such words as blatant criticism of himself and his ideas, which he considered absolute heresy. Mao became increasingly suspicious of those around him and determined more than ever to resist leaders like Liu Shaoqi, who were busy

Liu Shaoqi pictured with his wife. Mao would work behind the scenes to try to discredit Liu in order to attain total control over the Communist Party and China.

undoing the damage of the Great Leap Forward. To Mao, the new leaders were not trying to correct his mistakes; they were undermining his leadership.

Jockeying for Power

The appointment of Liu Shaoqi and the demoting of Mao left a power vacuum. Other high Chinese Communist Party officials began to jockey for power and favor. Party politicians resorted to rumor, intrigue, flattery, jealousy, and backbiting to curry favor with Mao or Liu. The smallest matters would be built up into major issues. Careers would be built—and ruined.

Three of the most vicious—but skilled—players at this power game were actively trying to restore Mao to unrestrained power and to increase their own personal authority. They were former secret police chief Kang Sheng, Mao's wife Jiang Qing, and defense minister Lin Biao. Their scheming would eventually result in the violent upheaval known as the Chinese Cultural Revolution.

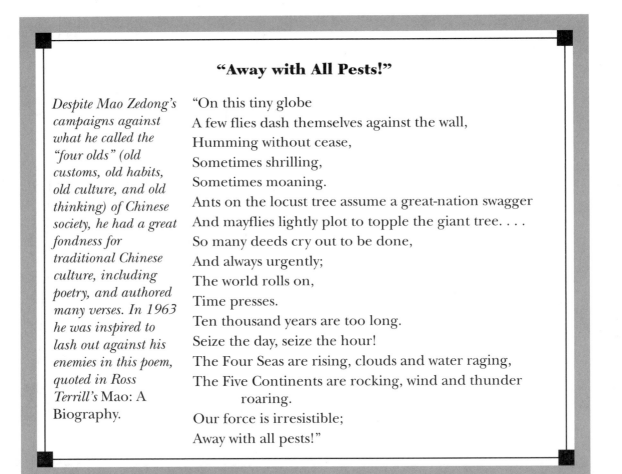

"Away with All Pests!"

Despite Mao Zedong's campaigns against what he called the "four olds" (old customs, old habits, old culture, and old thinking) of Chinese society, he had a great fondness for traditional Chinese culture, including poetry, and authored many verses. In 1963 he was inspired to lash out against his enemies in this poem, quoted in Ross Terrill's Mao: A Biography.

"On this tiny globe
A few flies dash themselves against the wall,
Humming without cease,
Sometimes shrilling,
Sometimes moaning.
Ants on the locust tree assume a great-nation swagger
And mayflies lightly plot to topple the giant tree. . . .
So many deeds cry out to be done,
And always urgently;
The world rolls on,
Time presses.
Ten thousand years are too long.
Seize the day, seize the hour!
The Four Seas are rising, clouds and water raging,
The Five Continents are rocking, wind and thunder roaring.
Our force is irresistible;
Away with all pests!"

The King of Hell

Of those helping Mao plan his comeback, perhaps the most clever and sinister was Mao's former chief hatchet man Kang Sheng.

Kang had risen rapidly in the leadership of the Communist Party by brutally routing out spies, opponents, and potential rivals. John Byron and Robert Pack wrote in *The Claws of the Dragon:* "The methods he popularized in Ya'an shaped public security [secret police] work through the Cultural Revolution and beyond."[13]

After Japan's defeat, when civil war broke out between the Communists and Nationalists, Kang was assigned to a task he had little experience in: land reform. Again he used the most inhumane methods to do his job; he resorted to publicly humiliating, torturing, and killing landlords. Landlords were buried alive, nailed to walls, or frozen in subzero temperatures. Whenever Kang entered an area, he found that those Communists previously in charge of the land reform program had not been diligent enough. His real purpose, however, was not land reform; his intention was to crush any opponents he might have in the party and to increase his own power.

Kang went too far. His party rivals convinced Mao that Kang should be demoted to heading the local party in his native Shandong province. The demotion was a huge setback for Kang, and he reacted by pretending to be seriously ill and withdrawing from all public life.

Starting in 1956, however, he began a comeback, deciding that his path back to power would again depend on currying favor with Chairman Mao. Unlike many

One of the most feared men in China was Kang Sheng. His reputation for using torture, humiliation, and murder to enforce slavish devotion to Mao made him an effective ally.

other top Chinese leaders, Kang supported Mao's hundred-flowers-blossom movement from the beginning, perhaps sensing it was all a trick to smoke out opponents. By 1958 Kang regained his place in the party's top leadership.

Kang goaded Mao into acting against his rivals. The brutal Kang was a skilled and smooth schemer with Mao. "Kang poisoned Mao's mind with the notion that Chinese society must be purified of all reactionary and revisionist elements," wrote John Byron and Robert Pack in *The Claws of the Dragon.*[14]

Jiang Qing

In Ya'an many years earlier Kang Sheng had used his friendship with Mao's fourth wife, former actress Jiang Qing, to win the leader's favor.

In the late 1920s when Jiang took up acting she also became involved with the CCP. In 1933 she moved to Shanghai and became active in the Communist Youth League, resulting in her arrest by the KMT. Whether she betrayed other Communists is still a mystery, but she did sign a confession, was released, and became less active in the CCP. Coincidentally or not, her acting career grew.

When the Japanese overran Shanghai, Jiang's world came crashing down. Fleeing the city and determined to find adventure, she sought to renew her Communist connections in Ya'an.

Jiang and Mao soon fell in love, but the couple faced some serious obstacles. Mao was still married to his third wife; in addition, he was twenty-one years older than Jiang. Jiang's shady political past also posed problems for a future relationship as well. In the highly suspicious world of Chinese Communist politics, anyone who had once been arrested by the Nationalists was considered a potential KMT spy.

At this point Kang Sheng became influential. Jiang knew Kang and because they were both from Shandong province, they shared a special bond. "With Kang Sheng as a dependable friend," she remarked, "no enemy can really hurt me."[15]

Kang realized that Mao desperately wanted to marry Jiang. At one point Mao threatened to leave the Communist movement and take up farming if he could not have her. No one was sure how serious he was, but many high party leaders still opposed the match. They received word from CCP members still in Shanghai that Jiang was a suspected KMT "secret agent."[16] If Kang, however, could produce proof that Jiang had not betrayed fellow Communists to the KMT, the path to a Mao-Jiang marriage would be cleared.

Kang did his work well. He destroyed incriminating documents and forged others. Jiang and Mao could be married, but other CCP leaders (including Liu Shaoqi) insisted on one important condition: Jiang would not appear publicly as Mao's wife, and she would be barred from political activity for thirty years.

It was not an easy bargain for Jiang to make. She thought she should play a key role in her nation's revolution, perhaps even as a top CCP leader.

Mao and Jiang married in 1938. In the 1950s she brooded over Mao's loss of face following the Great Leap Forward. Along with her old ally Kang Sheng she began plotting her husband's return to unbridled power.

It was Jiang's strategy to pore through official state and party documents and published articles looking for ways to influence Mao. She would point out any real or imagined attacks on his leadership and push him to gain unlimited power.

In 1962 Jiang made her first public appearance. Soon she would be taking an aggressive part in the struggle against Mao's rivals.

Lin Biao

Kang Sheng and Jiang Qing played vitally important roles in encouraging Mao, but for Mao's return to absolute power to succeed he would need more than encouragement and backroom scheming. He would need the force of arms, which neither Kang nor Jiang could provide.

China's defense minister, Lin Biao, also attempting a political comeback, could provide the arms.

Early in his political career, Lin was part of the Moscow-dominated wing of the party, opposed to Mao's theories of peasant-based guerrilla revolution, but he distinguished himself on Mao's Long March, and Mao came to respect his military genius.

After fighting began against the Japanese, Lin won one of the Red Army's few

" 'New China' Had Become Corrupt"

Mao and his clique preached socialism and equality but lived like petty tyrants. Their hypocrisy sickened those around them, including Mao's longtime personal physician, Dr. Li Zhisui. He wrote in his memoir The Private Life of Chairman Mao:

"I certainly did not like Jiang Qing—her decadent life of luxury and leisure, her pretending to be ill when her health was as good as mine, her constant bossing and pushing people around, her incessant impossible demands. She was as bad as the evil landlords of an earlier era whom the party vociferously attacked. But I had grown up to hate hypocrisy around me, the communist leaders' public carping against the corrupt bourgeois life-style of their predecessors, the touting of their high and lofty moral principles, while they themselves were living lives of luxury as the masses suffered and toiled and died. My hopes and dreams, my visions of Mao and of the new good society, were shattered for good.

Jiang Qing was wrong in assuming I still revered Mao. My adulation of him had dissipated too. What lofty moral principles did he follow? He had cast aside Peng Dehuai, one of the country's great revolutionary leaders, as if he were garbage, and he was gathering young women around him like the most degenerate of ancient emperors. And the Chinese people? The Communist Party had taken 'the people' and praised them to the sky while these very people were being oppressed and exploited, forced to endure every hardship, accept every insult, merely to survive. 'The people' were nothing but a vast multitude of faceless, helpless slaves. This was the 'new society,' the communists' 'new world.' Jiang Qing was right that I was disgusted with her. But I was disgusted with her husband too, with all of Group One [the leadership]. 'New China' had become corrupt."

victories against the foreign invaders. In 1938, however, Lin was seriously wounded and had to be removed from active command. He was sent to Moscow to recover and remained there until August 1941.

When he returned home to China, Lin quickly adjusted to changing political conditions and curried favor with Mao. Lin still praised Stalin and the Soviet system but wisely added that "the Communist Party of China will make equal progress under the leadership of Comrade Mao."[17]

Lin busied himself with studies of Marxism and military strategy and played little role in the fight against Japan. When

Through skillful direction of the military, Chinese defense minister Lin Biao was able to aid Mao in his desire to regain control of China. He was among the first to turn devotion to Mao into an almost fanatical cult.

war resumed against the Nationalists, however, he was more than ready for action and oversaw the CCP's tremendous victory in the Chinese civil war.

Lin commanded Chinese forces in the Korean War against UN forces in the early 1950s, but before that war was over, he returned to China. He had developed into an extreme hypochondriac—afraid of contact with water, sunlight, and wind. He became deathly afraid of sweating and feared that too much activity might harm his health. Like Kang Sheng and Jiang Qing, Lin Biao spent a good part of the 1950s outside of the People's Republic inner circle of power.

Decades before Lin had opposed Mao, but now he realized the key to his future was in slavishly following, indeed virtually worshiping, him. "The mass cult of Mao-worship," wrote Martin Ebon in *Lin Piao*, "was perfected by Lin within the army before it was extended to the whole nation."[18]

Kang Sheng, Jiang Qing, and Lin Biao were at the heart of those urging Mao to regain control. They were powerful, resourceful, and determined to succeed. Arrayed against them were some of the ablest leaders the CCP had produced—Defense Minister Peng Dehuai, President of the People's Republic Liu Shaoqi, and general secretary of the CCP's Central Committee Deng Xiaoping.

That Little Man over There

Assisting Liu Shaoqi in rolling back the mistakes of Maoist radicalism was a man who would eventually emerge as one of China's great leaders: the four-foot-eleven inch-tall Deng Xiaoping.

Deng Xiaoping walks among Chinese Communist Party delegates. Mao would consider Deng a major impediment in his quest for total power.

Deng had joined the CCP in 1923 while he was a student in France. When he returned to China in the late 1920s, he distinguished himself as a military commissar (an official assigned to a military unit to ensure loyalty to party principles and policies) and later as a party bureaucrat in southwest China. In 1952 he was named as one of China's five vice-premiers, and in 1956 Deng became general secretary of the CCP, a position of immense importance. He was then, and had been for years, a loyal follower of Mao in battles within the party.

His future looked bright. In 1958 Mao pointed out Deng to Nikita Khrushchev: "See that little man over there? He is very intelligent and has a great future ahead of him."[19]

Deng was too intelligent not to see that the Great Leap Forward was a huge mistake. He began doubting Chairman Mao's wisdom and sided with Liu Shaoqi in downplaying Mao. "A donkey," said Deng about the Great Leap Forward, "is certainly slow, but at least it rarely has an accident."[20]

By January 1965 Mao decided not to tolerate Deng's and Liu's revisionist policies any longer, although he would still give his old comrades some opportunities to mend their ways.

They didn't change, and the Cultural Revolution was about to begin.

3 The Cultural Revolution Begins

The stage was now set for a power struggle of epic proportions as Mao attempted to regain complete power. Mao had never lost all of his power. He had suffered a setback after the Great Leap Forward, but he still held a share of authority. Mao remained CCP chairman and had tremendous influence in society. His popularity among the rank and file was still immense. Even many who would later be falsely accused of anti-Mao activities had so much respect for Mao they would force themselves to believe that these charges must somehow be correct—because the great Chairman Mao could not possibly be wrong.

Liu Shaoqi also had his share of power. He was president of the People's Republic and held great influence over governmental policy. Mao resented having to share authority with Liu and his supporters such as Deng Xiaoping. In fact, he resented having to share power with anyone. He wanted to be absolute ruler of China once more—and he would go to any lengths to do so.

Mao had resourceful allies in his war against Liu and Deng. Helping him were Jiang Qing, Kang Sheng, and Lin Biao. Lin had influence in the armed forces; Jiang was growing more influential in the nation's cultural life, and Kang was skilled at using intrigue, ruthlessness, and false accusations.

What was really at stake was political power, but Mao's supporters hid their real agenda. They claimed that Liu was attempting to restore capitalism to China—that he was turning his back on true communism and true Maoism. While it was correct that Liu was unwilling to follow Mao blindly into such disasters as the Great Leap Forward, it was not accurate that he was attempting to restore capitalism. Yet as the power struggle grew, such charges became more common and seemed more believable to millions of Chinese.

Plunging into Chaos

Under ordinary circumstances a power struggle within the Communist Party would be violent enough. Millions of people might be expelled from its ranks. Thousands might be executed. However, in the 1960s the rivalry between Mao and Liu would lead to the great proletarian Cultural Revolution and spill over from within the Communist Party into Chinese society as a whole. The Cultural Revolution would soon degenerate into mob violence of unprecedented proportions, plunging China into ever deepening chaos.

Reading Between the Lines

Many of the Cultural Revolution's most hotly contested issues may seem strange to us. High officials lost their jobs because of their opinions about characters in plays or even reviews of those plays. Other high officials haggled over the content of operas or movies. These arguments hid the fact that the real struggle was over power. The public debate took such odd forms because the Chinese people traditionally had little freedom of speech or expression and often disguised what they were really talking about. When the Chinese spoke about a play, they might actually be talking about Mao or his opponents.

The Dismissal of Hai Jui

The struggle between Mao and Liu finally burst into the open in November 1965 when Jiang Qing and Kang Sheng, along with their supporters in the Chinese press,

"Faith and Good Works Go Together"

In the years after the Cultural Revolution, people in the West have become increasingly aware of how ruthless Mao really was. Nevertheless, at one time, many Westerners naively believed that Mao was a great social reformer. Among these observers was New Zealander Maslyn Williams. In his 1967 book The East Is Red, *he wrote almost mystically about the powers of Maoism.*

"Mao has much significance: as a modern philosopher of international significance, a political and military strategist, a genius, a myth (many expert Western 'observers' believe that he is dead). You may take your pick.

I would suggest that he has been a most successful modern missionary, preaching once again that faith and good works go together. I would suggest, too, that the achievements of his preaching and teaching present not so much a threat but a challenge to the West, and especially to Western Christianity; that if Christianity is not soon revitalized it will not long survive, for our Western world, troubled in conscience and in mind, cries out for the guidance which religion does not give, and Christ crucified is no longer justified in the works of his church.

But the Chinese believe that Mao . . . has freed their spirit and given them a dignity for which they are prepared to pay with sacrifice of self and service, far beyond any that we of the West seem willing to make."

launched a series of literary criticisms of a play written by an ally of Liu Shaoqi.

The play, *The Dismissal of Hai Jui*, was written by Wu Han, the deputy mayor of Beijing, and was about an emperor of China who dismissed a high official. The Maoists claimed that it was actually a rebuke of Mao for having dismissed Defense Minister Peng Dehuai six years earlier. In September 1965 Mao himself criticized Wu Han's play and its supposed attacks on his leadership. "The crux of the play," Mao explained, "is the question of dismissal from office. The Ming emperor . . . dismissed Hai Jui. In 1959 we dismissed [minister of defense] Peng [Dehuai]. Peng is Hai Jui too."[21]

Mao's attempt to regain power started by attacking several officials who had allegiance to his rival, Liu Shaoqi. One of the first to be attacked was Peng Zhen (pictured), the powerful mayor of Beijing.

Wu Han's play was not an attack on Mao. Mao, in fact, had personally suggested Wu Han's topic, but facts were of little importance when high-stakes politics were being played. Wu Han resigned from his position. Next, the Maoist forces went after Wu Han's boss, the powerful mayor of Beijing, Peng Zhen, an even closer ally of Liu Shaoqi. They accused Peng Zhen of supporting Wu Han's literary attack on Chairman Mao. Peng Zhen, however, was not the real target of the Maoists—no more than Wu Han had been. Liu Shaoqi and Deng Xiaoping were.

Trouble was brewing. "There was the smell of gunpowder in the air," recollects Communist Party activist Zhao Wenhao. "Something serious was going to happen. Everyone had that feeling."[22]

Military Coup

The key to Mao's being able to regain his prominence, however, was not the party or cultural criticisms but rather control of the three-million-man People's Liberation Army (PLA). PLA chief of the general staff Luo Ruiqing, a friend of Liu Shaoqi, held immense influence. Luo had to be removed for Mao's bid to crush Liu to succeed. After all, as Mao had pointed out in 1938: "Every Communist group must grasp the truth: 'Political power grows out of the barrel of a gun.'"[23] The PLA had the guns.

Luo Ruiqing had long been at odds with Lin Biao and Mao. Luo supported a more structured army; Lin and Mao favored guerrilla warfare and reliance on sheer Marxist-Leninist enthusiasm. "Luo," noted John Byron and Robert Pack in *The*

Claws of the Dragon, "became a symbol of resistance to Mao's concept of the military, as well as to Lin Biao's control over the PLA."[24] It was obvious that Luo would have to go if Mao's plans were to succeed.

On December 8, 1965, Luo was in South China when he received word to return to Shanghai for an important meeting. When he reached that city, he noticed his subordinates were ominously quiet. Then he was led to a curtained limousine and taken to a secret location.

Luo was now a prisoner. Lin Biao began a ceaseless interrogation of his former commander, hoping to force a confession of disloyalty out of him. A week later Luo was charged with being a counterrevolutionary, stripped of all his offices and formally placed under house arrest. Shortly afterward he fell—or was pushed—from a sixth-floor window. The fall did not kill him, but his troubles were not over. A decade of Maoist persecution, including internal exile and harsh living conditions, awaited Luo. With Luo out of the way, Lin Biao took total control over the army.

Lin Biao now spread the rumor that several of Liu Shaoqi's supporters planned to overthrow Mao (the February mutiny). Using the rumor as an excuse, in March 1966 Lin moved the thirty-three-thousand-man Thirty-Eighth Army into Beijing as a "protective force."

Mao now openly declared that if Peng Zhen and his allies in the Beijing Communist Party Committee and in various propaganda departments continued to protect persons such as Wu Han, he would destroy them.

On May 16, 1966, the Politburo fired Peng Zhen from all his official posts. "Peng's fall," observe John Byron and Robert Pack, "represented a crucial step as Kang and his allies moved to gain power over the entire country."[25] Kang's next victims would be Liu and Deng.

Nie Yuanzi's Big-Character Poster

In order to make trouble for his rivals, Mao also tried to create student unrest. He was always a revolutionary and thrived on chaos and struggle. China's university students were eager to provide Mao with the shock troops he needed to generate that chaos.

Just as Wu Han had met his downfall because of a play, China's students would be stirred to a Maoist frenzy because of a poster.

In Chinese universities, one of the few ways students or teachers could publicly express themselves was to create and display so-called big-character posters. These posters proclaimed revolutionary slogans—such as Long Life to Chairman Mao or Death to the Imperialists—in big characters (the Chinese language does not have letters but instead thousands of characters) and were displayed on public streets and buildings. As in all other modes of expression in the PRC, the big-character posters had to support official CCP positions. Even the slightest disagreement from the party line could endanger a poster's author.

Nie Yuanzi was head of Beijing University's philosophy department. On May 25, 1966, she and six of her students posted a big-character poster attacking the university administrators and other pro–Liu Shaoqi party functionaries. The radical clique around Mao wanted to report news

Big-character posters like this one were one of the few ways the Chinese could express themselves, being denied access to free speech. One such poster would figure prominently in the fight for power between Mao and Liu.

of Nie's actions in the country's newspapers and radio broadcasts, but Liu's supporters still had enough power to block such actions. Finally on June 1, Mao ordered the People's Republic newspapers and radio stations to tell the Chinese people about Nie's poster. Mao's decision was an unmistakable signal to the party and the people at large that Liu Shaoqi was in serious political trouble.

Nie Yuanzi's big-character poster became merely the first of many increasingly harsher public attacks on Liu Shaoqi's faction. The Cultural Revolution was off and running. As the Maoists gained strength, scores of Liu's supporters were forced out of office.

The Fall of Liu and Deng

On July 18, 1966, Mao, his power growing each day, returned to Beijing. Liu Shaoqi tried to retain control of what power he had left. He convened a plenary, or full, session (the eleventh) of the Eighth Central Committee, thinking that he could easily control the gathering and that it would support his position. He was wrong.

"The 'Royalists' Have Panicked"

The beginning of the Cultural Revolution was heralded by the posting of the first big-character posters. This editorial from the June 4, 1966, issue of Beijing's People's Daily, *as reprinted in the Asia Research Centre's* The Great Cultural Revolution in China, *describes the excitement the posters created.*

"There is today a vigorous revolutionary situation in Peking University. The poster put up by seven comrades, including Nie Yuanzi, written in big characters, was the opening shot. Everyone in the university was inspired and there was widespread joy as soon as the contents of this poster was broadcast on the radio and published in the newspapers. The proletarian revolutionaries are elated and the ranks of the Left have rapidly expanded. Tens of thousands of big-character posters have descended on the heads of the anti-Party and anti-socialist elements like a rain of shells. The active support given by all universities and colleges in Beijing has greatly enhanced the revolutionary power and prestige of the proletariat. The 'royalists' have panicked, they have become completely isolated. Under the leadership of the work team sent in by the new Municipal Party Committee, the students, faculty members and workers are firmly settling things and combating anti-Party and anti-socialist crimes of [university chancellor] Lu Ping and the others. . . .

The situation in our country is excellent. The people of the whole country have boundless love for Chairman Mao and the Central Committee. . . . Mao Zedong's thought has penetrated people's minds, the political consciousness of the masses is higher than it has ever been and tremendous successes have been registered in the socialist revolution and construction. No one who opposes Chairman Mao, Mao Zedong's thought, the Party's Central Committee, the dictatorship of the proletariat or the socialist system can escape the censure and condemnation by the whole Party and the whole nation, whoever he may be, whatever high position he may hold and however much a veteran he may be. The only possible result is his total ruination."

At the session Lin Biao charged that two of Liu's top officials, Minister of Culture Lu Dingyi and secret police official Yang Shangkun, were attempting a coup d'état.

Using this alleged plot as an excuse, Lin Biao had his troops seize Beijing's radio stations and public security positions. With such key offices under his control, his own military coup was gaining strength.

Liu Shaoqi now realized he was in a precarious position. He decided to publicly admit his errors and in that way perhaps avoid even worse trouble. "I myself caused this trouble," he told the party leadership, hoping they would leave him alone if he made this confession, "and I cannot blame you if you have complaints against me."[26]

The Merciless Kang

Liu Shaoqi again guessed wrong. In normal times, China's leadership might have accepted such a confession and allowed Liu to live in peace. Years before, the disgraced Kang Sheng was merely demoted to a provincial position. This time, however, the vicious and merciless Kang was on the other end of the purging process, and Liu's words merely triggered greater and greater attacks upon him. On August 18, 1966, Kang Sheng gave the orders: "Please organize Red Guards to investigate the renegades who infiltrated every unit and department. Investigate the question of the arrest and treachery of Liu Shaoqi and others."[27]

That month Liu was demoted from the position of second ranking party member. A year later a mob beat Liu so mercilessly that his leg was broken.

Meanwhile Mao's clique was also targeting Deng Xiaoping for destruction. Mao resented Deng's recent aloofness toward him and complained: "At meetings he would sit far away from me. He has not reported to me about his work since 1959."[28] Mao knew the reason for Deng's remoteness was that he was siding with Liu Shaoqi against Mao.

Deng had hoped to avoid a fall from power by changing sides and by not opposing Mao when the chairman purged Deng's old friends Liu, Wu Han, and Peng Zhen. That strategy came too late to save Deng. "In sacrificing Peng Zhen, [Deng] hoped to appease Mao and to contain the extent of his radical enterprise," wrote

Once Mao was able to cast doubt on the loyalty of Liu Shaoqi (pictured), Kang Sheng worked to completely humiliate and discredit him.

"*Everyone* Believed He Had Committed Mistakes"

The great proletarian Cultural Revolution began with a great deal of popular enthusiasm. Thanks to Chairman Mao's personal popularity, many supported his efforts to rid the party of his opponents. In Enemies of the People, *Anne F. Thurston quotes Wang Hongbao, son of a high-ranking party official, as he recalled how people felt in the early days of the Cultural Revolution.*

"When people tell you they were always opposed to the Cultural Revolution, that they never supported it, you must not believe them. You must ask them more. Because when the Cultural Revolution began, everyone supported it. Ninety percent of the people supported it—even those who were accused, even those who came under attack.

My father was one of the very first people to come under attack, right after Wu Han, right after the purge of the [Beijing] Party committee. And my father believed he was wrong. He believed he had committed serious mistakes. He came home one day and told us that. He said that he had not committed mistakes intentionally, that he had not realized at the time that they were mistakes, but that still he had made mistakes. But he said that he had always supported Chairman Mao. We must not blame anyone for what was happening to him and for what would happen to him. I came to believe that the attacks against my father were warranted.

Mao's status was very high; his authority was very great. He was like a god. Nothing he said could be contradicted. Everything he said was right. So when he and others said my father had committed mistakes, I believed them.

And that's another thing. *Everyone* believed he had committed mistakes. The old intellectuals believed they had committed mistakes. You should have seen them. They were all confessing to their mistakes. Even Liu Shaoqi wrote his self-confession. So when people tell you they never believed they had committed mistakes, you must not accept it."

German author Uli Franz in *Deng Xiaoping*. "How mistaken he was!"[29]

By December 1966 the press was filled with attacks on Deng. They branded him as the "number two capitalist roader," just behind Liu in wanting to return to capitalist ways, and called him a Khrushchev-type revisionist Communist.

By now, many of Mao's opponents were given death sentences or were being beaten to death in struggle sessions (a practice in which persons were beaten, harassed, and forced to admit their political and personal faults). Mao shielded Deng from both fates, but the chairman did not protect him from other punishments that were now routinely handed out to those who had run afoul of Mao's wrath. Deng was paraded around city streets with a dunce cap on his head. He was also forced to humiliate himself by confessing his misdeeds at huge public rallies. The onetime powerful party leader was now reduced to earning his living at a factory finishing the rough edges off screws.

The Death of Liu Shaoqi

The Chinese Cultural Revolution would soon match the French and Russian revolutions in massive cruelty—as Liu Shaoqi would soon find out. As the symbol of resistance to Mao, Liu Shaoqi would have to pay a high price for having incurred the chairman's wrath.

The brutal beatings that Liu suffered in August 1967 took their toll on his health. It took him an hour to perform such simple tasks as putting on his clothes or walking less than a hundred feet. His guards were forbidden to give him any help. The meals he received were sporadic and consisted of hard buns and poor quality rice. With only seven teeth left, the aged Liu had difficulty chewing his food. "His body grew weak," wrote Anne F. Thurston in *Enemies of the People*. "His hands trembled. He had difficulty bringing food to his mouth. It spilled on his body and face."[30]

By the summer of 1968 Liu had developed pneumonia. Doctors treating him aggravated his condition by subjecting him to further violent and demoralizing struggle sessions. They finally recommended he be hospitalized, but authorities rejected the suggestion.

Liu was now so weak that he could no longer feed himself and had to receive sustenance through a plastic tube. On November 24, 1968, Liu's seventieth birthday, his former associates notified Liu that he had been expelled from the Communist Party over a month earlier.

Liu remained in this weakened, half-alive state for another year. On October 1, 1969, Lin Biao ordered that Liu and other disgraced former top party officials be moved from Beijing to a prison in Kaifeng. In the cold autumn air, the aged and weak Liu was covered only by a threadbare blanket. Again, he contracted pneumonia.

On November 12, 1969, Liu finally and mercifully died. For three years not even his family was informed of his demise. A full decade passed before the people of the People's Republic learned that their former president was no more.

Liu was not the only person to receive such brutal treatment. It was typical of what was handed out to thousands and thousands of other party officials purged during the Cultural Revolution.

Jiang Qing's War on Culture

Jiang Qing fought the Cultural Revolution through the nation's arts and culture. Mao's wife banned operas and plays that recounted the exploits of emperors or ancient heroes. She mandated that Chinese

In a Jiang Qing–inspired production called Red Guard Soldier *an image of Mao appears onstage at the end of the performance. Jiang tried to develop the cult of Mao by using Chinese literary and cultural achievements to disseminate propaganda.*

art had to serve the Maoist revolution by glorifying the party, the workers, and the peasants.

First Jiang formed the League of Left-Wing Dramatists that promoted plays featuring heavy Maoist propaganda. Then she staged a Festival of Beijing Opera on Contemporary Themes, consisting of thirty-seven new revolutionary operas in Beijing's Great Hall of the People. The idea was that these operas and plays should be about revolution and class struggle rather than about the old themes of "emperors, princes, generals, ministers, scholars, and beauties, and on top of these, ghosts and monsters."[31]

Many officials, particularly Peng Zhen and Deng Xiaoping before their fall, resisted Jiang's efforts. Deng dismissed Jiang's productions as "a bunch of people running to and fro on the stage. Not a trace of art."[32]

Her operas were indeed boring and clumsy pieces of political propaganda, but that didn't stop the former actress's efforts to control more and more of the country's cultural institutions. By 1965 she was interfering in the Central Philharmonic Society.

She announced that Western-style symphonies were "dead."[33]

Yet her big break was yet to come. In 1966 her new ally Lin Biao named her as special advisor to the arts for the People's Liberation Army (her influence over the army had been minimal). Through the arts, Jiang would pass on her vision of radical Maoist revolution to millions of young Chinese military personnel. "She was to be chief advisor to an army of three million," noted Ross Terrill in *The White-Boned Demon*, "on opera, dance, music, and novels. She was to wear khaki fatigues as the male officers did. The job put Jiang into the mainstream of political power."[34]

Saving the Revolution

The Cultural Revolution was founded on the high, if often unrealistic, ideals of the Chinese Communist revolution such as freedom from foreign domination, personal equality, and better living conditions for workers and peasants. Yet the high-sounding goal of preserving the revolution would be accompanied by violence, cruelty, and brutality. The cruel death of Liu Shaoqi was just part of the brutality that would engulf China. To save China, the great proletarian Cultural Revolution would nearly destroy it.

4 Red Guards, Red Terror

The Red Guard student movement played a key role during the Cultural Revolution. The Red Guards were a paramilitary Maoist youth group made up of young people, often teenagers who pledged fa-

Members of Mao's Red Guard march in Beijing in 1966. The Red Guards carried out Mao's dirty work by punishing dissenting citizens in China and in return received power and privileges from Mao.

natical devotion to Chairman Mao and his thoughts. The Red Guards saw Mao as a vehicle to achieve power. The group became Mao's battering ram, a way to find out which people were disloyal to him and punish them.

In May 1966 the Red Guards were formed at Beijing's Qinghua University. The group started out protesting the school's administrators, who had been appointed by the Liu Shaoqi administration. Mao encouraged this and other rebellions that created the Red Guard movement. "Bombard the headquarters," he said, referring not only to the enemies in the party hierarchy, the "party power holders who take the capitalist road,"[35] but also to all authority except his own. The Red Guards soon moved out from the campuses and into the mainstream of Chinese society. They sought out Mao's enemies—both real and imagined—and dealt with them in the most savage ways.

Our Five Red-Categories Parents

The Red Guards at first restricted membership in their units to students of the five red categories, that is, to those groups that by their very nature were thought to be revolutionary: those young people whose parents had been workers, peasants, members of the PLA or revolutionary cadres (had belonged to the Chinese Communist Party before 1945), and revolutionary martyrs, or those who had suffered from KMT repression in bringing about the Maoist regime. These students from "good" worker or peasant backgrounds (the old, oppressed classes) had a great deal of animosity toward those from "bad" or more bourgeois backgrounds (representing the oppressors). Students with five red-categories parents were literally admitted through the front door of classrooms while those from bad family backgrounds were admitted through the rear door—if they gained entrance at all. At Beijing's Norman Bethune Blood Donation Station, Red Guards forcibly prohibited those from bad social backgrounds from donating blood and contaminating others.[36]

One article written by Red Guards from the Beijing Aviation Institute explained:

> What makes us Chairman Mao's Red Guards . . . is due to the fact that we are the sons of workers, poor and lower-middle peasants, revolutionary cadres, revolutionary army cadres, and revolutionary martyrs. . . . Who created history? Who pushed society toward progress. . . . Who conquered the world? Our five red-categories parents have done these things.[37]

Jealousy by these five red-categories students toward those from older prerevolutionary upper-class backgrounds helped create vengeful, discriminatory behavior. During Liu Shaoqi's reforms, more bourgeois students had been allowed greater freedom within China's educational system—and did better in school than the five red-categories students. The Red Guard movement was as much an envious attack on them as it was on Liu Shaoqi's clique or anything else.

Black Red Guards

While membership in the Red Guards was first restricted to students of the five red categories, students from bourgeois backgrounds soon formed their own Red Guard units. These students, from the so-called five black categories (which included children of former estate owners, rich peasants, antirevolutionaries, and rightists), had several motivations. Some were genuinely swept up in the enthusiasm of the Cultural Revolution and believed in its goal of a new Chinese society. Others, however, realized that the Red Guards were a new source of power and wanted to gain some of that power for themselves. Some students may have joined in self-defense. If they did not attach themselves to Red Guard units, they might be branded as counterrevolutionaries and hunted down and persecuted by other Red Guards.

In order for the black Red Guards to prove themselves redder than the red Red Guards, they often engaged in some of the most extreme behavior of the Cultural Revolution. Their outrages, however, did not win them any friends among the proletarian Red Guards. Adrian Hsia wrote in *The Chinese Cultural Revolution:*

> The proletarians were prepared to go to any lengths to keep the bourgeois out of the new movement, which

As a Red Guard propaganda truck moves through the streets, blaring Maoist philosophy from its speakers, children swarm around it. Such trucks were just one way the Red Guard was used to inspire loyalty to Mao.

would have effectively eliminated them as professional rivals, whilst the bourgeois, for their part, were prepared to engage in revolutionary activities of the most extreme kind in order to safeguard their university and career prospects.[38]

But the proletarian-bourgeois split in the Red Guards was not the only cause for dissent among the Red Guards. Soon even proletarian Red Guards began denouncing each other as counterrevolutionary and battled each other physically. They also attacked elements of the party leadership, not even sparing the radical wing led by Jiang Qing.

Clearly the Cultural Revolution was spinning wildly out of control.

Red Guard Rallies

At the center of the Cultural Revolution were the huge Red Guard rallies held in

"We Will Smash the Old World to Smithereens"

At the massive August 18, 1966, Red Guard rally at Beijing's Tiananmen Square, radical university professor Nie Yuanzi was among the speakers praising Chairman Mao. As quoted in The Great Cultural Revolution in China, *she stated:*

"A Great Proletarian Cultural Revolution without parallel in history is being carried out in our country under the leadership of our great leader Chairman Mao. This is a revolution of world significance. We will smash the old world to smithereens, create a new world and carry the Great Proletarian Cultural Revolution through to the end.

Sailing the seas depends on the helmsman, the growth of everything depends on the sun, and making revolution depends on Mao [Zedong's] thought. We heartily wish long life to our most respected and beloved great leader Chairman Mao. We shall follow Chairman Mao's teachings, pay attention to state affairs and carry the Great Proletarian Cultural Revolution through to the end. We will certainly follow Chairman Mao's teachings, face the world and brave the storms, and become most reliable successors to the revolutionary cause of the proletariat.

Chairman Mao is the reddest sun in our hearts. The Chinese people's revolution has never been all tranquil without storms and waves. We shall bear Chairman Mao's teachings firmly in mind, and temper and test ourselves in great storms and stresses. We will defy death to defend the Party's Central Committee and Chairman Mao. We face a mountain of swords and a sea of flames, but we also have a great beacon light—Mao [Zedong's] thought which will surely guide us to victory.

Chairman Mao stands among us. This is the happiest and most important moment in our lives. We'll read his works, follow his teachings, act according to his instructions and be his good pupils for the rest of our lives."

Beijing. Starting in August 1966, crowds of more than one million Red Guards from all over China would gather at Beijing's Tiananmen Square to hear speeches by Chairman Mao and by his supporters such as Lin Biao and Jiang Qing.

In the Cultural Revolution's early stages its leaders hoped that every Chinese secondary and college student might visit Beijing to pay homage to Mao and to the bold new world of the Cultural Revolution. That ambitious goal was never met, but eleven million provincial Red Guards did visit Beijing.

The crowds at these rallies would reach a wild frenzy of enthusiasm for Mao, virtually worshiping him in much the same manner as Germany's Nazis had gathered to praise their leader, Adolf Hitler. For many participants seeing and hearing the great Chairman Mao was the high point of their lives. Red Guards would return home from these rallies with increased determination to rout out all opponents of Mao and of themselves.

Red Guard Activities

All across China various Red Guard detachments formed to smash the old, non-Maoist way of life. The names of typical Red Guard units—Victory or Death, the Scarlet Guards for the Defense of Mao Zedong's Thought, Struggle-Unto-Death to Defend Chairman Mao Combat Corps, and Mao Zedong Thought Fighting Regiment—illustrated how fanatical they were and how much they idolized Mao. Mao was the center of their universe.

The Red Guards, acting with support of radical Maoist government and party officials, demanded that each public building display Mao's portrait and maintain a collection of his writings. The Guards directed that everyone should be familiar with Mao's thoughts and use them as guidance not only politically but also in their daily lives.

Strict rules governed how Mao's image could be displayed. Almost every private home reverently displayed Mao's picture. His four-volume *Selected Works* and the little red book *Quotations from Chairman Mao*

also were given honored places in each home. Over 740 million copies of *Quotations from Chairman Mao* were printed during the first two years of the Cultural Revolution.

The Red Guards attacked anyone they thought to be bourgeois (that is non-Communist or Western middle class). Part of their behavior was based on the old Communist Party practice of forcing false confessions out of its enemies. Other portions came from traditional Chinese forms of humiliation. The Red Guards paraded their victims at rallies and on public streets, making them wear dunce caps on their heads or embarrassing placards around their necks. Dunce caps have a special meaning to the Chinese because that is what the souls of the condemned wear in hell for all eternity. Confessions of the wearer's guilt or insulting personal references were written on the placards, which were made of heavy slate, the kind school blackboards are made of. The placards' weight made the wearers double over in great pain. All the while the Red Guards shouted at their victims, blew whistles in their ears, and rang gongs to make them confess to anti-Mao thoughts and crimes. A hail of punches and kicks accompanied the noise. The Red Guards didn't want their fun to end too soon; they wanted their victims to confess at just the right time. Confessing too quickly would only incite Red Guard mobs to greater violence.

Becoming a Red Guard Enemy

Eventually over twenty million Red Guards rampaged across China during the worst days of the Cultural Revolution from 1966 through 1968, moving from town to town, creating chaos as they fought against non-Maoist and traditional-minded people. Often Red Guard members simply used the Cultural Revolution as an excuse to lash out at their own personal enemies.

In their rivalry to prove who was most loyal, the Red Guards intensified their attacks on other Chinese. They burned books that were thought to be Western or bourgeois. The Red Guards raided private homes in search of anything smacking of the four olds, or worse, for proof of collaboration with the West or with Chiang Kai-shek's exiled, but still feared, Kuomintang. They destroyed art treasures from the past or from the capitalist West, including those found at Beijing's Central Academy of the Arts. These priceless collections were vandalized—unless they found their way into the private collections of such high party officials as Kang Sheng, who fancied himself an artist and was noted for

Red Guard members use public humiliation to discredit members of "anti-revolutionary groups" by making them wear dunce caps that proclaim their "crimes." Such tactics cut down on opposition to Mao.

"You Couldn't Trust Anybody"

Any totalitarian system creates dangerous feelings of mistrust and suspicion, and the Chinese Cultural Revolution raised such attitudes to new levels. In Feng Jicai's Voices from the Whirlwind, *an anonymous factory worker told his story.*

"I'm sure they planned to persecute me. The excuse was something I'd said. In fact, it was just a joke. When I was drinking with some guys I worked closely with, I made a wisecrack about how the first Ming emperor suddenly killed all his loyal followers when he got himself on the throne. That got reported to the factory leaders as a slight on Chairman Mao. You couldn't trust anybody in those days. I didn't know until the next night, March second, 1968, that I'd been reported, and suddenly I found myself being denounced in a mass meeting as a counter-revolutionary. Instantly, big-character posters went up all over the place. . . . I was ferreted out! According to the posters, my family background had changed to a capitalist one instead of worker. Therefore I was planning a 'class revenge.' I don't know who wrote that stuff, but everyone jumped on the bandwagon. No way I could argue. At first it was only denunciation, but then the military representative shouted the slogan 'Verbal struggle, no violence!' It was a prearranged signal. A bunch of [them] jumped me and began beating me really badly. They used angle irons and all kinds of things that were lying around. I couldn't tell who was attacking me; all I knew was to cover my head with my handkerchief and hands. I didn't bleed a lot; there was a hell of a lot of sharp pain. I was almost killed. They all came down on my head. . . . I'm still half deaf in one ear from that beating and I hear a ringing sound all the time. I passed out from their kicks and punches. They tied me up with steel wire and sent me to the police."

his vast personal collections of illegally obtained art.

The Red Guards hated anything foreign, not just foreign politics or films or music. Anyone who had worked for foreign companies fell under suspicion of being an enemy of the revolution. Red Guards burst into people's houses and berated them for eating foreign foods such as jam or drinking foreign beverages such as coffee. They once attacked the children of a man who had worked for a Swiss

Mao and Lin Biao in the midst of a Red Guard rally in Tiananmen Square in 1966. Mao used the Red Guards to dampen dissent and keep his name prominent in the minds of the Chinese people.

fingers broken so he could no longer play so skillfully. Those being interrogated were constantly insulted and made to go for days without sleep. Photos appeared in the newspaper of Red Guards carrying baskets of human ears and noses, which had been chopped off their victims' faces. Many victims of the Cultural Revolution committed suicide rather than face any more torture, humiliation, and persecution.

Deprived of Humanity

Red Guards accused one man of being a capitalist because he rented out a spare room in his house to a boarder. They smashed everything in his home. He and his family were beaten with belts and then dragged out to the street and humiliated further. Then they were brought back into their house and left without food for days on end. After finding a pen knife in the ruins of their house, they desperately decided to commit suicide. The family's daughter was a doctor, and it was agreed she would kill her parents first and then herself. She killed her father, but then Red Guards burst in. She and her mother jumped out of a window. The mother soon died, but the daughter, despite two broken legs and miserable treatment in prison hospitals, survived. She was sentenced to life in prison for her father's murder but was released in March 1979. She still lives with the guilt of her act. "In the Cultural Revolution," she told an interviewer, "people were deprived of their basic humanity. Who in their right mind could stab her own father to death? Under normal circumstances no one would even consider it."[40]

company as "puppies of the running dog of Swiss imperialism,"[39] (Communists often called their enemies "running dogs") and forced them to help burn their father's books.

In order to humiliate those with special talents or skills the Red Guards often employed grotesque cruelty. One brilliant speaker and debater literally had his tongue ripped out to silence and humiliate him. The son-in-law of a prominent official who won fame as a concert pianist had his

Hong Yung Lee wrote in *The Politics of the Chinese Cultural Revolution*:

On the whole, the attitudes of the Red Guards were arrogant, authoritarian and coercive, reflecting a mentality that went along with their privilege and high position in society. Advancing the slogan "Long Live the Proletarian Uprising," they subjected the "class enemy" to physical abuse and torture in their private jails and torture rooms.[41]

The Name Game

Not all of the Red Guards' behavior was violent. Some was merely overly zealous and enthusiastic, such as the renaming of factories, shops, and streets to rid the People's Republic of what the Red Guards considered to be dangerous Western or bourgeois influences. For example, in Beijing the old Handley Watch Shop still retained the name of its former foreign owner, even though it had long been owned by the state. One day, the Red Guards arrived, tore down the shop's old iron sign, and renamed it the Capital Watch Shop.

"We thought that iron name would be hard to remove," boasted one Red Guard, "but the workers gave us tools and when we hit the iron with their heavy mallets it cracked very easily. It was just another paper tiger."[42]

The Red Guards' efforts to rename city streets failed to go quite so smoothly. Competing Red Guard units would rename different parts of streets with different names, or they might give the same popular revolutionary name, such as "Anti-Imperialist" or "The East Is Red," to many different streets in the same city. Before long hardly anyone knew where anything was anymore.

The same need for order would soon lead to the end of Red Guard violence.

Chapter

5 The Tide Turns

As Red Guard–created chaos spread from one corner of China to another, resistance sprouted up almost immediately. That was not surprising. To begin with, not everyone in China's power structure fully supported Mao's lust for power and violence. Because of Liu Shaoqi's influence, many government officials were not affiliated with Mao's wing of the CCP. Even if the Red Guard movement had not degenerated into mindless violence, these officials would have had little enthusiasm for the youthful radicals.

These moderates—and others like them in the party, in the PLA, and in society at large—looked upon the violence and destruction of the Cultural Revolution with disgust. Some fought back.

As early as August 1966, Chinese civilians retaliated by killing particularly vicious members of Red Guard detachments. Such activity was previously unthinkable and showed just how rapidly the People's Republic was moving toward civil war and outright chaos. The following month in Chingtao, forty thousand workers banded together to fight roving Red Guard bands. Similar battles occurred in almost every other large Chinese city, often pitting Beijing Red Guard units who had virtually invaded an area against local workers, peasants, and party and government offi-

cials who wanted Red Guard lawlessness simply to go away.

As the Red Guards became more vicious in their attacks, the military began to have doubts about the riotous atmosphere the Red Guards were creating. Some army units cracked down on leftist Red Guards, but most did not. Mao still shielded the Red Guards from any retaliation by the army.

That attitude changed after a particularly serious incident in Wuhan, a major industrial area of China, where two pro-Maoist Red Guard factions battled. The local PLA commander, Chen Zaidao, intervened on the side of the relatively more moderate of the two factions. The other faction appealed to Beijing for help. Two high officials flew to Wuhan and ordered Chen Zaidao to clamp down on the moderates. Chen surprised everyone by arresting them.

On the Verge of Chaos

China seemed on the verge of degenerating into chaotic battles between regional military leaders, or warlords, who ignored Mao and the nation's central government. The idea of a new warlord era in Chinese

A young Guardsman shouts during a 1966 rally. The Red Guard split into many small factions and often battled each other on the streets of China's cities. The lack of control among the Red Guard would lead Mao to distance himself from the group.

history shocked authorities in Beijing. Quickly the party leaders ordered the army and navy to blockade the Wuhan area. Paratroopers seized the region's main airport. Premier Zhou Enlai himself flew in and persuaded General Chen to surrender. Chen and his close associates were flown back to Beijing where they suffered severe beatings at the hands of Red Guards and agents of Kang Sheng.

At first it seemed like the Wuhan incident was a victory for the radical Red Guards and a defeat for the military lead-

ers who wanted to control them. Actually, the exact opposite reaction took place. The Wuhan incident showed that the army was essential in maintaining order, and when it acted, no other power in China was strong enough to oppose it. It also demonstrated that many people within the army and within the population at large opposed the radical Red Guard agenda. Although Chen Zaidao had been personally defeated, his cause lived on. "The Wuhan warlord's cause won," [43] noted Ross Terrill in *Mao*.

"Our Object Was to Humiliate These People"

Not surprisingly, public opinion soon turned on the Red Guards and their destructively cruel behavior. Dai Hsiao-ai, a Red Guard from a Canton secondary school who later defected to Hong Kong, told his story in Stanley Karnow's Mao and China.

"In practice, we confiscated things like vases and furniture decorated in the traditional way. If there were revolutionary objects, like pictures of Mao [Zedong], we left them alone. Usually, we would smash something just for effect and confiscate everything else. . . . We took all foreign-made items, like blankets and quilts from Hong Kong as well as jewelry, scrolls, and even books that had been published before 1949.

Because we were afraid that people would hide things, we searched their homes very thoroughly. Some of us would tear down the walls and look behind the plaster while others seized shovels and picks and tore up the cellars looking for hidden items. . . .

While we searched each house, we made the occupants stand to one side while a few members of the group shouted that they must confess their counterrevolutionary crimes. If the women had long hair, we cut it. Sometimes we would shave half of the hair on a man's head and defy him to shave the rest. Our object was to humiliate these people as much as possible. . . .

Statues, paintings and other such objects in public parks, temples, and cemeteries were quickly destroyed. We had no plan on these occasions, but simply roamed the streets looking for things. Someone would shout, 'Let's go to such-and-such temple,' and we would all follow. Very often, some other group would have been there first and left nothing but a pile of ashes or a group of statues smeared with paint. At least once a day, we would cart a statue to a large intersection and ceremoniously smash it to pieces. Passersby would stop and watch us. Some would congratulate us, but most lowered their heads and hurried by."

Yet the PLA was still not allowed to act nationwide and was afraid to move on its own. It bided its time against the Red Guards. The army waited and patiently watched China dissolve into anarchy. If the situation grew bad enough, Lin Biao and his allies reasoned, Mao would have no choice but to turn to them to save China. Hong Yung Lee observed in *The Politics of the Chinese Cultural Revolution*:

[PLA leaders] intentionally neglected the PLA's tasks so that the social order was disrupted, communication and transportation systems came to a standstill, and consumer goods became scarce on the market. They made some concession to the rebel [radical] forces, for instance by allowing the rebel forces to seize outdated weapons, while willingly supplying more sophisticated weapons to the conservatives.[44]

Rampaging Red Guards even disrupted China's foreign policy. In January 1967 they occupied the Ministry of Foreign Affairs and sent insulting cables to foreign nations, leading to embarrassing incidents with such countries as Burma and Cambodia. Not satisfied with this outrage, for two weeks in August 1967, thousands of Red Guards surrounded the Soviet embassy and screamed anti-Soviet slogans into loud speakers to insult those inside. In the summer of 1967, Red Guards burned the British embassy in Beijing to the ground, mistreating its employees and making them bow to a giant portrait of Chairman Mao.

The Arrest of Chen Yi

Radical young people even arrested premier Zhou Enlai and threatened to put him on trial. Mao agreed but only on the condition that he stand with him. Zhou was freed after a few days. Red Guards also arrested foreign minister Chen Yi and interrogated him relentlessly. All the while, though, he remained foreign minister of the world's largest nation. Chen rarely lost his composure. Red Guards made him wear a dunce cap during his interrogations but allowed him to take it off at other times. He asked if he could wear it while eating lunch as he had grown rather fond of it, but not all of Chen Yi's associates were as tough. One killed himself rather than continue being subjected to threats, ridicule, and torture.

Finally, Mao complained, "[Chen Yi] has lost twenty-seven pounds. I can't show him to foreign visitors in this condition."[45] He ordered the mistreatment of Chen Yi to stop.

"I Am the Black Hand"

In the summer of 1967, Kang Sheng realized that Mao was getting nervous about Red Guard violence and determined to trick the Guards into taking actions that would cause Mao to turn against them. Kang goaded Kuai Dafu, a leader of an ultraradical Red Guard unit at Qinghua University where the movement had begun, into additional confrontations with the PLA. The confrontations made Mao reconsider his support of the Red Guard movement.

Mao did not act, though, until a year later. By now the wily Kang Sheng had distanced himself from the Red Guards. That July, no doubt operating on Mao's orders, Kang bluntly warned Red Guard leaders that they had gone too far in spreading mindless chaos across China.

Do you know who you're making happy? The American imperialists, the Soviet revisionists, the traitors, and special agents—that's who you're making happy. You shout about wanting revolution. . . . Some of you have reached the edge of the cliff. One more step and you'll go over.[46]

Just two days later Mao summoned five prominent Red Guard leaders, including Kuai Dafu and Nie Yuanzi, the originator of the big-character posters.

Mao was angry over the Red Guards' continuing use of violence and the chaos it had created. Kuai, however, didn't at first realize how upset Mao was and complained how powerful party members had interfered with the Red Guards. Mao made it plain the party was working on his orders. "I," he bragged, "am the black hand that suppressed the Red Guards."[47]

Mao scoffed at the Red Guards' military strength and made clear who really held power in the People's Republic. All he had to do was give the word, and the Red Guards' freedom would vanish. "[The Red Guards'] cannon fodder is limited in number . . . ," Chairman Mao mocked. "How can that be compared with the number of troops under Lin Biao?"[48]

Red Guard Members Exiled

The Red Guards soon learned how serious Kang and Mao were. The two now began to show the Red Guards who actually controlled China and for whom the Cultural Revolution was really being run—Mao, Kang, and their inner circle.

Mao exiled huge numbers of Red Guard members to China's remote countryside. If they resisted, they were shot. In the winter of 1968–1969, Mao expelled twenty to thirty million Red Guard students from China's cities. Their internal passports, needed for travel within the People's Republic, were revised and barred them from urban areas. Their city ration cards were revoked. The PLA rounded up Red Guards and sent them off by the truckload and trainload to the countryside, as far away from the centers of power as possible.

Once in the countryside Red Guards found themselves enrolled in special

Mao addresses Red Guards in Tiananmen Square, chastising them for creating chaos and asking them to go to the countryside and help with the harvest. Mao's words were put into action when the military exiled huge numbers of Red Guard members to the countryside.

"How My Classmates Envied Me!"

Even with the Red Guards retreating, loyalty to Chairman Mao was absolutely essential, and an enthusiastic display of that devotion was equally important. One way to show that loyalty was by sporting a Mao badge. A former high school student, speaking anonymously in Feng Jicai's Voices from the Whirlwind: An Oral History of the Chinese Cultural Revolution, *described how important the wearing of such a badge was in 1969.*

"It was the nicest badge I had. The kind of badges we were wearing at the time were called, in the jargon of those in the know, 'the eighty-round steamships.' 'Eighty-round' referred to the fact that the diameter of these badges was eighty millimeters, about the size of a *shao bing* [a flat sesame-seed cake, popular in northern China]. These 'eighty-round' badges were the largest available. The size of these badges mattered in that the larger they were, the more loyal the wearer supposedly was—and certainly the more startlingly visible they were. The 'steamship' referred to a steamship tossing in a windswept, stormy sea, whose helmsman, of course, was Chairman Mao, without whom the ship would be lost. Of these badges, the image of the Chairman and the ship itself were copperplate that shone with a luster like gold. Behind the ship, above the sea, was a large red sun. The badge itself was coated with a layer of the kind of bright paint found on the five-star badges that were pinned to caps at the time. All in all, these 'eighty-round' badges were the newest, largest, and most fashionable of their kind at the time. There was not the slightest doubt that they were works of great craftsmanship. Stealing glances at the 'eighty-round' badge pinned to my clothes, how my classmates envied me! Especially pleased with myself, believing myself to be the most loyal to the cause, I would walk proudly with my head held high, with more than a touch of exhibitionism."

schools. There they were to learn from the peasants and refine their study of Chairman Mao's thoughts. In truth, these schools were nothing more than prison camps, where former Red Guards lived in peasant huts and worked in slave-labor conditions. "The real purpose of [these schools]," observed Dr. Li Zhisui in *The Private Life of Chairman Mao*, "everyone knew, was not learning but punishment."[49] Once-prominent Red Guard leaders such as Nie Yuanzi and Kuai Dafu found themselves enrolled in such schools.

Even those Red Guards not sent to the countryside could become targets of Mao's reaction to their violence. "Workers'

"A Beacon Light Guiding the Whole Army"

Lin Biao was an early practitioner of the cult of Chairman Mao, as this excerpt from an article entitled "The Army and the People Throughout the Country Are Determined to Master Mao Zedong's Thought" reprinted in the Asia Research Centre's The Great Cultural Revolution in China *illustrates. It also reveals how the Mao cult could easily be transformed into a Lin Biao cult.*

"Comrade Lin Biao has made higher demands on the whole army in the creative study and application of Chairman Mao's works at a time when the Great Proletarian Cultural Revolution has come to a high tide and a new situation and a new order of things have appeared in the study of Chairman Mao's works by the whole Party and the whole nation. This shows his great concern for the political developments of all cadres and fighters. This is a beacon light guiding the whole army in studying Mao Zedong's thought well and in its advance along the road to thorough proletarianism and militancy. . . .

Filled with their boundless love for Chairman Mao, the commanders and fighters of the army units spare no efforts to pass on Comrade Lin Biao's instructions to the masses of the people near where they are stationed. One army unit under the [Beijing] Command has organized 36 propaganda and cinema teams which have made lantern slides of Comrade Lin Biao's instructions to carry out propaganda in the area of Hsingtai, Hopei Province. Many army units under the Wuhan Command have sent out a large number of instructors to make Comrade Lin Biao's instructions known among the masses of the people. The commanders and fighters of the army units seize this chance of conducting propaganda among the masses to learn from the local activists in studying Chairman Mao's works, acquainting themselves with their outstanding deeds and experience so that they can do a still better job in organizing study in their own units."

Mao Zedong Thought Propaganda Teams," composed of PLA members and ordinary workers, took control of the universities. The workers, jealous of the students' special privileges and resentful of the Red Guards' arrogant behavior, were particularly harsh and vindictive. "When the workers would come to lecture us they'd unbutton their shirts and prop their feet up on the tables,"[50] recalled one former senior Red Guard in Feng Jicai's *Voices from the Whirlwind.*

Other Red Guards faced arrest on trumped-up charges. That same senior

Red Guard quoted above told how authorities unjustly arrested his roommate for writing a pro-Mao wall slogan that someone else had turned into an anti-Mao slogan. Fellow Red Guards paraded him around the city in humiliating fashion before sentencing him to ten years in prison. Another fellow student had accidentally splashed some ink drops on a portrait of Mao. The picture was discovered, and he also received a ten-year sentence. "It was really scary," the anonymous senior Red Guard recalled, "even worse than the white [Kuomintang] terror before Liberation."[51]

The People's Liberation Army Rules

With the Liu Shaoqi–Deng Xiaoping faction still disgraced and the Red Guards exiled to the countryside, Lin Biao's PLA gained increased prestige not only in the government but also in virtually the whole of Chinese society. People's Liberation Army members staffed government agencies. More and more PLA officers took over provincial Chinese Communist Party operations. Military units, known as "army units to support the left," fanned out to each province, supposedly to promote the revolution but actually to crack down on Red Guard troublemakers. The army units ended up running the provincial governments. By August 1971 twenty of the twenty-one provincial CCP first secretaries were members of the PLA. PLA propagandists provided instruction to the masses on how to best study the thoughts of Chairman Mao. Millions upon millions of ordinary Chinese party members and citizens all wore baggy green People's Liberation Army uniforms as they tried to conform to the new order. Dr. Li Zhisui noted in *The Private Life of Chairman Mao*:

> With Lin Biao approaching the height of his power, all China was becoming militarized. Charged with restoring order to the country, the army had taken control of government offices and work units at every level of Chinese society.[52]

A Lin dynasty even started to appear. Lin's wife, Ye Chun, won appointment to the Politburo, a rare honor for a Chinese woman, and Lin's young son, Lin Liguo, became deputy director of the Air Force Command. Collections of Lin Liguo's speeches were printed and made available to the public. Air force members proudly proclaimed their loyalty not only to Mao and Lin Biao but to Lin Liguo as well.

Yet while Mao had used Lin Biao and the People's Liberation Army to restore order and control the Red Guards, he never intended for the army to control the Chinese Communist Party. Years ago Mao had warned, "Our principle is that the Party commands the gun, and the gun must never be allowed to command the Party."[53] Lin Biao would soon learn what that meant.

6 The Death of Lin Biao

The most chaotic phase of the Cultural Revolution had come to an end when the People's Liberation Army gained control of the Red Guards. The PLA's rise also meant increased influence for the already powerful Lin Biao. Many Chinese homes now not only contained a portrait of Chairman Mao but also one of Lin reverentially displayed next to it. Clearly, the masses—who knew who held power in China—looked to Lin and the PLA for guidance.

At the Chinese Communist Party's Ninth Party Congress, held on April 14, 1969, Lin reached new heights. Before that meeting he had been second in the party only to Mao, but China's constitution now formally named him as Mao's political heir. Never before had a successor to Mao been so designated. It was a great triumph for Lin, but as an old proverb goes, Be careful what you wish for, you just might get it.

Being Mao's successor marked the beginning of the end for Lin Biao. Chairman Mao began to resent him and the increased control the army was exercising over China. Until this point Mao had encouraged and supported Lin; now, he would cut Lin back down to size. As author Ross Terrill observed in his biography of Jiang Qing, *The White-Boned Demon:*

"In 1970 it was Lin who discovered that being number two meant living in a cell for the condemned just as Liu Shaoqi had done in the early 1960s."[54]

Our Friends

Some of Lin's problems stemmed from his stand on foreign policy matters. With true revolutionary zeal Lin had long advocated guerrilla-style warfare against the imperialist West, particularly the chief capitalist nation, the United States.

But the world situation was changing. Relations between the People's Republic and the Soviet Union continued to worsen. Beijing charged that in June and July 1969 alone Moscow instigated 429 armed clashes along the Sino-Soviet border. When Soviet premier Aleksei Kosygin visited Beijing in September 1969, Mao rudely refused to meet him. Premier Zhou Enlai, who did confer with Kosygin, would allow him to go no farther on Chinese soil than the airport.

Mao needed help against the Soviets and realized that meant becoming friendlier with the world's other superpower, the United States. On October 1, 1970, he publicly announced that "Peoples of the

Mao and President Nixon shake hands during Nixon's unprecedented diplomatic mission to China in 1972.

world, including the American people, are all our friends."[55] Mao's message was a carefully chosen signal to America that China wanted the United States to help against the Soviets. Before long Mao, through the skillful diplomacy of Zhou Enlai, would be entertaining President Richard Nixon, a former anti-Communist hardliner, in Beijing and moving toward friendship with the imperialist, capitalist Americans.

In one sense this startling change was almost beyond comprehension, but throughout Mao Zedong's long career, and particularly during the Cultural Revolution, he had first allied himself with one faction of the Chinese Communist Party and then, as circumstances changed, with another. Now he was applying the same principle of ruthless opportunism to foreign policy.

Lin, however, was not as flexible, cunning, or intelligent as Mao. He clung to his old, rabidly anti-American ideas because his entire revolutionary global strategy would collapse if the "imperialist" Americans were no longer China's enemies.

Even worse, Lin secretly wanted to make peace with the Soviets, a move totally opposite to Mao's bold new initiative. Lin told his chief of staff, Huang Yongsheng: "Our new relation with the Soviets, the transition from war to armistice, hostility to alliance, secret contacts to open public relations, requires that great efforts be made to change the attitudes and beliefs of our people."[56] He was never able to carry through on his plan.

Lin was also plagued by horrible, often embarrassing, public-speaking skills, as when he confused "Pakistan" with "Palestine" in a speech, and by awkwardness in meeting with foreign, particularly European, diplomats.

Lin Biao seemed less and less worthy of leading China.

Lin Biao speaks at a rally in Beijing. Lin's often embarrassingly inadequate speaking skills and his odd personal obsessions would doom him to fall out of favor with Mao.

Geniuses and Presidents

Just as the Cultural Revolution had begun over the staging of a historical play, an issue that the rest of the world found mystifying, so the break between Mao and Lin came over two questions that seemed of little practical importance to outsiders.

The first controversy revolved around the idea of genius. By 1970 Lin had allied himself with Chen Boda, Mao's one-time speechwriter. At an August 1970 party conference held at Lushan, Lin and Chen proposed that the CCP recognize the concept of genius and further recognize that a genius of the magnitude of Chairman Mao came along only once every thousand years.

One might think this would have pleased Mao Zedong. After all, he had been virtually worshiped for over two decades. Yet he suspected Lin and Chen's motives and believed that their actions actually were designed to promote Lin and not himself. Mao fumed:

> There is someone who says genius appears in the world only once in several hundred years, and in China such genius has not come along in several hundred years. This does not accord with reality. There is somebody who says he wants to support me, elevate

me, but what he really has in mind is supporting himself, elevating himself.[57]

Mao clearly had begun to mistrust Lin and his ambitions, and the Plenum [conference] rejected the Lin Biao–Chen Boda idea of genius.

The second controversy involved the position of China's state presidency. Since Liu Shaoqi's downfall, the post had been vacant. Lin Biao recommended that Mao Zedong again occupy it, but in reality, he hoped Mao would turn it down and give the job to him. Lin was correct that Mao did not want the presidency, but he failed to realize that Mao would see through this scheme and that Mao did not wish for Lin to advance any further or faster than he

"He Had to Take Flight"

Lin Biao had his work cut out for him in challenging Chairman Mao, particularly when he turned to plotting his former patron's assassination. In The Private Life of Chairman Mao, *Mao's personal physician, Dr. Li Zhisui, wrote of the challenges Lin faced.*

"I do know that assassinating Mao was never going to be easy. Wang Dongxing [commander of the 8341 Corps] and his security personnel had seen to that. So had Mao. His plans were always secret, and changed so quickly and often that even his closest security personnel were kept off guard. Lin Biao's plans never stood a chance. When Mao returned safely to Beijing, Lin Biao knew that he had lost his war with Mao. He had to take flight. He knew the fate of others whose challenges to Mao had been less direct. I did not know then—but surely Lin did—that Liu Shaoqi had died in prison, from physical abuse, illnesses and medical neglect. So had many high-ranking leaders. Lin Biao's own death, once his plot against Mao failed, was certain. In the end Lin Biao ran out of time. . . .

In late 1971, when the Lin Biao affair was made public, the whole country was shocked. People within the highest reaches of the party were stunned. I was. I had known of Mao's reservations about the man everyone called the Chairman's closest comrade in arms and had been aware of an intense struggle between the two men since the Lushan conference of 1970, when Lin maneuvered to try to have himself declared chairman of the republic. The Cultural Revolution was vicious and vindictive, and many people died. But nothing prepared me for the extent of Lin Biao's perfidy or the drama of his final flight."

already had. Mao insisted the presidency remain vacant.

Lin and Chen Boda, nonetheless, still wanted to name a new president. Mao became infuriated. "Don't mention the question of president again," he angrily yelled at Chen Boda. "You want me to die earlier, so let me be the national president! Whoever wants to establish the presidency can be the president. Anyway I will not be."[58]

The controversy was a disaster for Lin Biao. His wife and three of his top generals were forced to make self-criticisms of their previous positions, admitting they made ideological errors. Chen Boda lost all his high posts and a month later was placed under house arrest.

The influence and power of both Lin and the PLA now stood on extremely shaky ground. Chairman Mao, always ready to strike down real or imagined opponents, moved quickly to limit the armed forces' influence.

"I Was Sweating"

Careful observers of the Chinese political scene could detect subtle but ominous signs that Lin was fast losing favor. For example, official toasts no longer included Lin's name. He no longer appeared at ceremonial occasions. Regional military commanders were shifted around in order to undercut Lin's power base.

Newspaper and radio stories contained veiled attacks on him, often warning against those like Khrushchev who had flattered Stalin when he was alive but turned on him after his death. Attacks on the idea of genius continued. "By pretending to acclaim someone as a genius," warned the newspaper *People's Daily*, "renegades from the Communist movement present themselves as 'geniuses.'"[59] To those familiar with the internal workings of the Chinese Communist Party leadership, such comments spelled trouble for Lin Biao.

But Lin's oddest bad omen was a photograph of himself reading *Mao's Selected Works*, taken by Mao's wife, Jiang Qing, a skilled amateur photographer. The photo, labeled "Tireless Student," was published in the popular magazines *People's Illustrated* and *Army Illustrated*. Ordinarily, this event would have been a very positive development, but Lin was bald and extremely sensitive about his lack of hair; he always wore a hat or cap to cover his condition. This photo showed him for the first time as baldheaded.

Embarrassed or not, Lin remained in the party's number two position, just below Mao. However, enemies surrounded Lin now more than ever. Kang Sheng, soon to die of cancer, had replaced Chen Boda in the number four party position and took over his role as head of China's propaganda ministry. He would skillfully work against Lin.

At the 1971 May Day celebration, a major holiday in the Communist world, an incident occurred that revealed to Mao how truly strange his handpicked successor was. Mao noticed that Lin arrived late for the ceremony. As important as Lin was, he was not supposed to be late at an occasion when Mao appeared. Respect for Mao demanded that the chairman always appear last; now Lin had unexpectedly appeared last, and Mao was not pleased. Lin, a hypochondriac, was terrified of such things as water, direct sunlight, and even of his own sweating. On May Day 1971 his

Mao and Lin Biao address crowds as Lin waves Mao's little red book. Lin's awkward plotting to overthrow Mao would lead to personal disaster.

sweating had sent him into a panic and caused his delay. Lin then had to explain why he was late to Mao. "I was sweating," he stammered.

Mao could barely contain himself. "Who doesn't sweat!" Mao slowly spat out one word at a time. Lin was flustered by Mao's enraged response and left the ceremony early, not even bothering to tell Mao why he had left.

Mao now thought his designated heir was not only too ambitious but also somewhat unbalanced—something he should have realized long before this. A few weeks later Kang Sheng, acting no doubt on Mao's command, began ordering the copies of *Lin Biao's Selected Works* found in government offices throughout China destroyed.

Code Name: 5-7-1

Lin Biao realized that unless he took drastic action, he might meet the same fate as Liu Shaoqi, Deng Xiaoping, and Chen Boda. Lin, who had once been unlimited in his praise of Mao, now privately told his friends that the chairman was "a paranoid and a sadist. . . . He is the greatest dictator and tyrant in China's history. . . . Those who are his greatest friends today will be his prisoners tomorrow." [60] Unlike Liu, Deng, or Chen, however, Lin had the armed forces, particularly the air force, behind him. Lin Biao now began to plot with his twenty-six-year-old son, Lin Liguo to kill Mao and seize power. Their plan was code-named 5-7-1 because the Chinese characters for "armed uprising" sound very similar to those numbers. Assisting Lin Biao and Lin Liguo were a number of high-ranking air force officers.

Their plotting was not very professional. They tried to kill Mao in a Beijing traffic accident. They poisoned his food. Mao's plane, with him aboard, was to be shot down by a Soviet-made, Chinese red flag missile, and Jiang Qing would be blamed for the deed. Mao's Shanghai mansion was to be strafed. Except for the shooting down of Mao's plane, Lin Biao and Lin Liguo attempted all of these plans; none succeeded.

Mao Suspects a Plot Against Him

Mao may not have been aware of all of these schemes or may not have been able to prove that Lin had been behind them, but the chairman became convinced Lin was plotting against him. He even believed Lin had caused him to develop a case of pneumonia. Mao's fears, particularly of poisoning, increased. In response, he resorted to ever more strict methods of security.

Words and signals meant a great deal in the secretive and conspiratorial world of Chinese politics. Until early September 1971, a huge, lighted sign hung over a branch of the People's Republic's only bank, the Bank of China. Until then it read "Long Live the Invincible Thought of Mao Zedong." Lin had carefully promoted an emphasis on Mao's thought rather than on Mao himself. That way Lin could assume the role of interpreting those thoughts.

When the sign was abruptly changed to read "Long Live Chairman Mao," Lin

As he began to suspect that Lin Biao (pictured) was plotting against him, Mao's fears increased.

knew that Mao was once again reasserting his authority. More importantly Mao planned on living as long as possible and preventing Lin Biao from assuming power in the near future.

On September 11, 1971, Lin Biao met with Lin Liguo and other top assistants to plot their most ambitious and complex strategy yet. Lin Biao called the plan the Jade Tower Mountain Scheme, and it would be triggered by an outbreak of fighting along the Sino-Soviet border on September 25. The fighting would then spread, create a national crisis, and cause the cancellation of October 1 ceremonies marking the anniversary of the founding of the People's Republic.

Using the fighting as a pretext, Lin would propose that three of his most loyal army divisions be stationed in the Western Hills near Beijing. He also would recommend that Mao and his top advisors retreat into the Central Committee's command center in the Jade Tower Mountain.

While this was going on, Lin would be in the Number 0 installation, a similar underground command post connected by a long tunnel to the Jade Tower Mountain.

At the proper time Lin's three army divisions would overpower the central garrison corps (code-named the 8341 Guards Unit) that guarded the Western Hills.

"The Agent of the Bourgeoisie"

After Lin Biao had died and the People's Republic media revealed his treachery, newspapers and radios left no stone unturned in attacking the leader they once hailed as second only to Chairman Mao. This excerpt from the Wenhui Daily *in November 1973 appears in Michael Y. M. Kau's* The Lin Piao Affair *(Piao is an older spelling of Biao).*

"In order to carry out anti-Party conspiratorial activities and practice revisionism, Lin [Biao] fanned up ill winds and wicked influences and attempted vainly to lure Communist Party members to become philistines and politicians by such nasty means as making promotions and promises, giving parties and feasts, and handing out gifts. The criminal conduct of this small handful of diehards has fully revealed that they were building the Party for capitalism and for private interests.

Lin [Biao] was the agent of the bourgeoisie within the Party spreading the rotten ideology and work style of the exploiting class. He and his like went all out to introduce the corrupt and dirty ill winds and wicked influences of the exploiting class into the Party in order to promote their counterrevolutionary revisionist line and subvert the proletarian dictatorship. In order to carry on counterrevolutionary conspiratory activities, they went so far as to put forth the so-called 'small matters are harmless' theory. In fact, they were for revisionism, for splittism, and for conspiracy and intrigue. The so-called 'harmless' fallacies were advanced only for the defense of their criminal conduct."

Then an assault team of Lin loyalists would pour out of the Number 0 installation, through the tunnel, and into the Jade Tower Mountain. Once inside they would kill Mao and all his supporters.

Lin Liguo helpfully suggested an improvement to his father's plot—pumping liquid fuel and poison gas into the Jade Tower Mountain complex before their assault troops invaded. "This way we can avoid some messy fighting," Lin Liguo said. "The annihilation will be cleaner—and more certain."[61]

Lin Biao approved. He told his chief of staff, Huang Yongsheng: "The exit to the underground Jade Tower Mountain installation will be sealed by my men, and before Mao has time to realize what is happening, gas bombs will have suffocated him. His body will soon be nothing but ashes."[62]

Part of Lin's plot involved keeping his involvement secret—even after the plan succeeded. Mao Zedong still had enough prestige that Lin Biao—even if he succeeded in murdering his former leader—was afraid to tell the Chinese people that he had done so. Instead, he would have Central Chinese Broadcasting Stations inform the world that a subversive group had attacked both Mao and Lin. Mao had died; Lin had miraculously survived. Only much later would Lin reveal that Mao had become a tyrannical monster and that Lin had been forced to eliminate him.

The Jade Tower Mountain Scheme fell apart because it was too complex. Arranging a border war with the Soviet Union, one of the world's superpowers, is not easily done. Lin soon abandoned the harebrained plan, but the fact that he had seriously considered it revealed how desperate he had become.

Death on the Train

On September 6, 1971, Lin Biao gave orders for a new plan. Lin Liguo would oversee the bombing of Mao's private train as it neared Shanghai, hitting it first with rockets and then with flamethrowers. Then, if Mao was still alive, an individual whom Mao trusted, Fourth Air Force Political Commissar Wang Weiguo, would board the train and personally shoot the chairman. Lin Biao would blame the murder on a rival military leader and proclaim himself the new head of the government.

Instead, the attack never came off. Mao arrived in Shanghai on September 10—before the conspirators were ready to strike. In Shanghai, Wang Weiguo attempted to board the train but failed.

Mao was now safely back in Beijing under the protection of Unit 8341. Time was clearly running out for Lin Biao, but he had a fall-back plan. He would head for Canton, lead a revolt, set up a separate government that could be recognized by foreign powers, and perhaps reach an agreement of some sort with China's official government. It was a long shot, but it was the only one Lin had left.

Lin had planned to fly to Canton on the morning of September 13 and had a plane waiting for him at the tiny Shanhaiguan airport.

Lin's conspiracy was uncovered before it began. Some researchers believe an officer revealed the plot; others say that Lin's own daughter reported it to Mao's associates. Still others contend that Zhou Enlai was keeping close tabs on Lin and learned that something unusual was in the air. Zhou found out about the plane at Shanhaiguan. He became suspi-

"A Serious Counterrevolutionary Affair"

Once a leader of the People's Republic fell into disgrace, everything had to be done to destroy his reputation. That included calling into question virtually every aspect of his life. In Lin Biao's case, that meant condemning his behavior decades before during the civil war against Chiang Kai-shek's Nationalists, as this Communique of the Central Committee of the Chinese Communist Party written in 1971 and quoted in Michael Y. M. Kau's The Lin Piao Affair *reveals.*

"It was not with a sudden change of mind that Lin . . . took the lead to organize a counterrevolutionary clique to oppose the Party and Chairman Mao. As early as the land reform period he already opposed Chairman Mao. During the period of the War of Resistance Against Japan [the Sino-Japanese War], he also made many speeches of complaint against the Party. During the War of Liberation period, he was engaged in building up an independent kingdom in the northeastern region behind the back of the central authorities. After liberation and from the time he took charge of the Military Affairs Commission, he did make certain worthy contributions to the Party and the state. Therefore the Party adhered to a policy of long-term assistance, education, and cultivation toward him.

However, Lin . . . belittled such assistance, education, and cultivation rendered by the Party. After the Ninth Party Congress, he . . . took the lead in organizing a counterrevolutionary clique in a wild attempt to oppose the Central Committee, to split the Party, and to establish another mountaintop. . . .

The Central Committee considers the series of conspiracies plotted by the Lin-Chen [Boda] anti-Party clique as a serious counterrevolutionary affair."

---

cious and ordered a military detachment to investigate.

Lin Escapes

By now Lin realized that his disloyalty was no longer a secret. He decided to flee the People's Republic and seek refuge in the Soviet Union. That night Lin, his wife, his son, a loyal air force general, and two assistants piled into a convoy of cars and headed for Shanhaiguan airport. Mao's troops were right behind. They fired at Lin's bulletproof Red-Flag-model limousine but failed to do any damage. Lin Biao's secretary (some say he was his bodyguard), Li Wenpu, resisted Lin Biao's attempt to flee. Lin Liguo pushed Li out of a car and shot Li in the right arm while he was on the ground.

When it became clear to Lin that Mao had discovered his plots to kill him, Lin tried to flee China in a plane. Lin and his family died when the plane crashed in Mongolia.

Lin's car outraced the troops in their slower military jeep, but more trouble awaited the Lins at the airport. With soldiers in hot pursuit, there was no time to fill up the plane with fuel. At best only a ton of gasoline was on board. While taking off the British-built, three-engine, hundred-passenger Trident grazed a fuel truck and damaged its right landing gear.

Word of this amazing sequence of events soon reached Beijing. Zhou Enlai wanted Mao to order missiles to shoot the Trident down. Mao refused. "Rain will fall from the skies," he responded. "Widows will remarry. What can we do? Lin Biao wants to flee. Let him. Don't shoot."[63]

There was no need to use missiles. Because Lin's plane was so short of fuel, its pilot attempted an emergency predawn landing 250 miles inside the Mongolian People's Republic, a Soviet satellite between China and the Soviet Union. On landing, its right wing hit the ground. The plane's fuselage broke apart, and its remaining fuel caught on fire. Either the impact or the resulting fire killed everyone aboard.

Some observers suspected that Lin's fiery death had *not* been an accident. One particularly fanciful story claimed that a 60-mm rocket ambush on Lin's Red-Flag limousine had killed both him and his wife. Some said that the bodies found in the crashed Trident were not those of the Lins. Others contended the bodies discovered were Lin and his wife but were riddled with bullets. Many believed Lin's Trident had been sabotaged. Why, they wondered, had Mao remarked so calmly on hearing that Lin had attempted to flee, "Let him go, he won't get far"?[64]

The truth, wrapped up to this day in the secrecy and deceit of Maoist China, may never be known.

The Secret Death

The Chinese government was afraid that other PLA leaders might also be disloyal and took some drastic steps in the wake of Lin's death. The government grounded all Chinese air traffic and, even more significantly to observers of People's Republic intrigue, canceled the October 1 celebration of National Day, the anniversary of Mao's seizure of power in 1949.

Yet the matter of Lin Biao's treachery and death was such an embarrassing and shocking issue that the party leadership

---

"Your Attitude Is Good"

A former Red Guard named Lo was accused of acting on Lin Biao's orders during the Cultural Revolution. He was taken to a prison camp in a remote portion of Jiangxi province in central China. There he was finally told he would be freed if he gave a statement admitting he had worked for Lin. He told his story in Fox Butterfield's China: Alive in the Bitter Sea.

"We had to rehearse it. First I had to memorize the whole thing, so there would be no mistakes when I spoke in front of the struggle session. They would tell me, 'This sentence you must say sadly. This paragraph you must say with real emotion.' In some places they wrote 'pause' for the other prisoners to talk. In other places they wrote 'slogans' so people could shout at me. Once I couldn't remember what came next. The guards said I was trying to cover up; actually I just forgot. Eventually they gave me the paper so I could read it.

The first time I was put in a struggle session, after fifteen minutes I felt numb, I was so scared. But eventually I got used to it. When they didn't beat me very hard, it was just like a pig going to market. Since my head was bowed and I couldn't see anybody, all there was was a lot of noise and shouting.

I never knew why [I was finally released]. They told me, 'You are an enemy of the people, but your attitude is good.'"

did not know how to reveal it to the Chinese people. After all, the Chinese population would wonder why their infallible chairman could make such a monstrous mistake as choosing the now-villainous Lin as his successor. If Mao had been wrong about Lin, a man he had worked with so closely for decades, what else might he be wrong about? The Great Leap Forward? The Cultural Revolution? Perhaps even socialism itself?

For a full two months, no one—not even party members—learned of Lin's death. At about that time, reports began appearing in the Western press that Lin was dead. Rumors constantly flew regarding Lin's whereabouts. Nevertheless, it was not until 1973 that the Chinese government informed its people that Lin Biao, the person most Chinese thought would be their next leader, had been dead for two full years.

7 China After the Cultural Revolution

The old guard was changing. In the 1970s Lin Biao was only the first of China's aging top leadership to meet death.

Kang Sheng was next. Kang, who had become seriously ill even before the Lin Biao affair, had begun plotting against Jiang Qing. He was too sick to carry his plan to completion and died on December 16, 1975.

Zhou Enlai, leader of the moderates, soon followed, dying of cancer on January 8, 1976. Mao named Hua Guofeng, a little-known official from Mao's home province of Hunan, as acting premier. Mao had supposedly given Hua a note reading, "With you in charge, I'm at ease."[65]

Hua was clearly a compromise candidate to succeed Mao. "Hua," noted Craig Dietrich in *People's China*, "was a combination Maoist, pragmatist, and opportunist with a certain bent for conciliation. He was tall, jowly, and rumpled in appearance, an obscure provincial functionary about to be thrust into the national spotlight."[66]

Deng Xiaoping would attempt to regain power in the early seventies, but China's powerful Communist Party was not ready to accept a moderate leader. He would not gain power until the late seventies.

The Return of Deng Xiaoping

While so many of his old comrades were dying, Deng Xiaoping kept returning from his political grave. In April 1973 dumbfounded foreign diplomats witnessed Deng at a reception given for Cambodia's Prince Norodom Sihanouk. In April 1974 he led a Chinese delegation to the United Nations. Nevertheless, the radical faction still retained great power. When Zhou Enlai died in 1976, some thought Deng was the logical person to replace him, but when Hua Guofeng became premier, Deng again mysteriously disappeared. Veiled attacks on him reappeared in the press.

In April 1976 over one hundred thousand persons gathered in Beijing's Tiananmen Square to pay tribute to the late Zhou Enlai, but tired of chaos and radicalism, the crowd soon turned to attacking Jiang Qing and praising Deng. When police cleared away their memorial wreaths for Zhou, the protestors rioted. Police killed

"70 Percent Right"

The People's Republic still grapples with how to treat the legacy of Mao Zedong. Should his crimes be fully revealed or should his reputation, even his worship, be restored? A. Dane Bowen in Foreign Service Journal *reported on how Deng Xiaoping and the Chinese leadership have taken a cautious, middle ground.*

"Once Deng Xiaoping had recovered in 1978 from his second fall from power, he launched a critical review of Mao, Maoism, and the whole Cultural Revolution. The official line came to be that Mao had been '70 percent right' although the new leadership publicly discussed more failures than would seem to fit into the '30 percent.' The Chinese Communist Party retained 'Mao Zedong Thought' as its guiding principle, while actually rejecting most of what was Maoism.

China has also resisted going along with the Soviet Union's de-Stalinization program; the authorities in China have never undertaken a re-appraisal of Stalin. On each May Day until the turmoil in 1989, the Chinese government erected huge portraits of the *lao zuzong* (old ancestors, or originators of communism) in Beijing's Tiananmen Square. The four were Marx, Engels, Lenin, and Stalin. China's official line on Stalin became the same as that on Mao, that he was about 70 percent right. Later there was some talk of perhaps 50 percent. . . .

Mao was the legitimizer of the regime and all policies that flowed from it, whether populism, anti-intellectualism, self-reliance, mass participation, or continued revolution. China's problem in exorcising Mao is that Mao is both the Lenin and the Stalin of the regime. A de-Leninization requires much more time, but it will come to China just as it has already started in the Soviet Union."

over a hundred of them and arrested thousands more before restoring order.

Deng lost all official offices and fled Beijing. He remained in hiding for the next few months but urged his fellow moderates to take action against their radical opponents. He asked:

> Are we supposed to stand here impotently waiting for them to slaughter us? Are we supposed to let four people [Jiang Qing and her allies, party vice-chairman Wang Hongwen, and two key attackers of Wu Han's play *The Dismissal of Hai Rui*, Zhang Chunqiao and Yao Wenyuan] set our country back a century? Or should we fight them as long as we have our breath? [67]

The Gang of Four

Death now claimed Chairman Mao himself. He had not been the same after Lin Biao's death. "The episode," Dr. Li Zhisui wrote in *The Private Life of Chairman Mao*, "left Mao depressed, listless, and unable to sleep. Finally, he became ill." [68] But depression was not his only malady. Increasingly weaker from amyotrophic lateral sclerosis (Lou Gehrig's disease), heart and lung disease (he had been a heavy smoker), and poor kidneys, Mao died just after midnight on September 9, 1976.

Two groups now jockeyed for position. One, led by Jiang Qing, oversaw the nation's cultural establishment machine but little else that could help it seize power. "Although they controlled the propaganda apparatus—the press, radio, TV, theater and cinema," observed John Byron and Robert Pack in *The Claws of the Dragon*, "they had no claim on the police or the military." [69]

Jiang Qing made her own bid for power after Mao's death. She was easily defeated, however, and ended up under arrest. She was tried as part of the Gang of Four and given a death sentence.

Hua Guofeng headed the other faction. Both cliques plotted coups, but Hua struck first. On October 5 the CCP's Politburo met to select a new leader. Jiang demanded to be named party chairman, but nothing came of the idea. Instead, the following night, troops from the 8341 unit arrested her associates, Wang Hongwen, Zhang Chunqiao, and Yao Wenyuan, as they arrived for a meeting at the People's Congress Hall on Tiananmen Square. Later that night police also stormed into Jiang's home and informed her that she too was under arrest.

Suddenly Jiang's power was broken. Mao had been right years before when he said, "Jiang Qing is a paper tiger. One blow and she is punctured." [70]

Hua Guofeng was now chairperson of the party, premier of China, and chairperson of the party's Military Affairs Commission, the nation's three highest positions.

His new government placed Jiang Qing, Wang Hongwen, Zhang Chunqiao, and Yao Wenyuan on trial.

The indictment against this Gang of Four ran twenty thousand words and accused them of wrongfully persecuting 750,000 persons—of whom 34,380 consequently died. Many of their victims were intellectuals. The Gang of Four was charged with harassing 142,000 persons in the Ministry of Education, 53,000 in the Academy of Sciences, and more than 500 of the 674 teachers in the People's Republic medical colleges.

All four were convicted. The court handed Jiang Qing and Zhang Chunqiao suspended death sentences. Peng Zhen, the once disgraced mayor of Beijing, had the pleasure of bringing Jiang news of her sentence. The other two members of the gang received long prison terms.

Deng Returns Again

The fall of Jiang Qing meant yet another comeback by Deng Xiaoping. Hua Guofeng opposed Deng's rehabilitation, telling him "you have committed errors and must therefore be criticized further."[71] However, in January 1977 over a million persons gathered in one-hundred-acre Tiananmen Square, the world's largest public square, to demand Deng's rehabilitation. Deng also enjoyed the friendship of many powerful officials, and in July 1977 Hua was forced to reappoint Deng to all the positions he had held before his second purge in April 1976.

Back in office, Deng took particular interest in promoting science, education, and technology, reversing the Cultural Revolution's paranoid suspicions of educated people. Deng complained:

> The Gang of Four made the absurd claim that, the more a person knew, the more reactionary he would become. They said they preferred labouring without culture and they praised an ignorant clown who handed in a blank examination paper as the model of a "red expert."[72]

Hua and Deng now moved even further apart, as Deng became a powerful symbol of reform. Much as the April 1976 crowds in Tiananmen Square supported Deng, the public again sprang to his defense. One highly visible part of this protest was the Democracy Wall on Beijing's Changan Boulevard that began in mid-November 1978. Big-character posters praising Deng and Zhou Enlai and criticizing not only the Gang of Four but also surprisingly even Mao himself covered the wall.

Things were clearly changing in the People's Republic.

Deng, who not long before had claimed he was satisfied to be "Chairman Hua's helper,"[73] now moved to attack Hua Guofeng's leadership and demand his ouster. In 1981 Hua was removed from office. Between three and five million hardline Maoists were purged from the party while Deng and his group of reformers (most notably party chief Hu Yaobang) began radically changing Chinese society. Deng permitted peasants to keep more of the food they produced. He placed greater emphasis on academic qualifications than on faithfulness to Maoist ideology in admitting students to universities. He moved away from heavy industry and toward the manufacture of more consumer goods. Most importantly, he imported capitalist ideas about profit and loss to China. Living standards improved dramatically. China's economy finally began to bloom. Chinese society took on a very different form of communism, and Maoism seemed at an end.

But economic reforms did not mean political reforms. The party still retained a tight hold on free speech and expression. In January 1987 fifty thousand people demanding increased liberty gathered in Tiananmen Square. The government did not give in and reacted by ousting Communist Party leader Hu Yaobang, who favored greater reform.

In September 1988 premier Li Peng, a Moscow-trained hard-liner, began a campaign of reining in China's reforms much to the displeasure of Hu's replacement Zhao Ziyang.

Tiananmen Square

By 1989 discontent over Deng's failure to open up China's political system reached the boiling point. "Virtually everybody," wrote Orville Schell in the introduction to *Children of the Dragon*, "was fed up with the rampant corruption, nepotism and favoritism that had invaded all branches of government."[74]

When former Communist Party leader Hu Yaobang, a symbol of reform, died on April 15, big-character posters appeared at Beijing universities urging a demonstration in his honor and large numbers of protesting students converged on Beijing's Tiananmen Square. Eighty thousand troops had to be called out to protect Hu's memorial service, while in the square

students chanted pro-democracy slogans and demanded that premier Li Peng come and meet them. In a dramatic visit Li and party leader Zhou Ziyang did talk with them. Zhou was conciliatory; Li was hostile and talked down to the protestors.

Before long more than 150,000 students had walked or bicycled to the square to confront China's dictatorship. "The Chinese government proclaims that democracy is here, but China still has dictatorship,"[75] said one protestor.

The student struggle quickly spread to other cities, including Shanghai, Nanjing,

In the 1980s, Chinese students held pro-democratic rallies in Tiananmen Square in hopes of a more open China. Their hopes were brutally dashed by the military.

"The Productive Energies of the Individual"

In the early 1980s Deng's reforms were transforming the Chinese economy— and Chinese society. Time magazine named him its 1985 Man of the Year. Time published this profile, "Deng Xiaoping Leads a Far-Reaching, Audacious but Risky Second Revolution," in its January 6, 1986, issue; it reveals how Deng's changes had revolutionized Chinese agriculture.

"The animating spirit of Deng's reforms has been to liberate the productive energies of the individual, a daring concept not just for a Marxist but for a Chinese (the concept of individualism has a negative connotation in Chinese society). He began, appropriately, with agriculture, which had been collectivized by Mao to a degree extreme even for the Communist world. The land was worked by communes that grew what the state directed and turned over all food produced to the state for distribution. Pay was based on a system of 'work points' that bore little relation to production: a peasant would accumulate a certain number of work points for planting rice seedlings, for example, but he or she would fare no better if the eventual crop was large than if it was small.

Deng's reforms abolished the communes and replaced them with a contract system. Though the state continues to own all land, it leases plots, mostly to individual families. Rent is paid by delivery of a set quantity of rice, wheat or whatever to the state at a fixed price. But once that obligation is met, families can grow anything else they wish and sell it in free markets for whatever price they can get.

Though the state retains the power to cancel a peasant family's lease and award it to someone else, that power is rarely exercised. Farm families are increasingly regarding the good earth as theirs and using it about the way they would if they owned it outright.

Farmers are allowed, indeed encouraged, to build privately owned houses on their state-owned land. Roads all over rural China have been narrowed by piles of bricks dumped along the shoulders to be picked up by peasants who are erecting homes or even paying others to do it for them. Compared with the days of Mao, when many peasants were required to live in dormitories and eat in communal mess halls, the change in life-style alone is almost revolutionary."

and Tianjin. Most of the rallies were peaceful, but in Xian, in northwest China, a rally turned into a riot. Twenty houses were burned; 130 police were injured.

By mid-May hundreds of thousands of students had gathered in Tiananmen Square, and they would not leave. On live television, millions of viewers around the world watched in rapt fascination as the drama unfolded. Would real democracy finally come to China, or would the People's Liberation Army swoop down upon the huge crowd and massacre it?

On May 20 Li Peng and People's Republic president Yang Shangkun declared martial law. Zhao Ziyang, often called the leadership's leading reformer, had not wanted to use force against the demonstrators and was ousted from his position. Shanghai mayor Jiang Zemin replaced him.

A Powerful Symbol

On May 30 demonstrators added a new twist. Protestors in Tiananmen Square had erected a thirty-seven-foot high, plaster and styrofoam "Goddess of Democracy," that bore a great resemblance to America's Statue of Liberty and was veiled in red, white, and blue cloth. The statue enraged the government but stood as a powerful symbol that democratic ideals were universal and united the Chinese and American peoples—indeed all peoples.

The standoff had continued for seven weeks. On Friday, June 2, 1989, the PLA finally made a brief attempt to clear the area peacefully. The demonstrators paid no attention. Tanks and troops returned the following afternoon. Soldiers lobbed tear gas into the crowd, whipping protes-

The Goddess of Democracy, created by Chinese students to symbolize their desires to move China toward democracy. The goddess would soon be destroyed, along with the students' hopes.

tors with belts and beating them with clubs. But the demonstrators held fast. Other persons from outside the square even rushed in to reinforce them. After more than five hours the troops retreated. Shortly afterward, twelve hundred soldiers returned. The demonstrators surrounded them, and the attackers soon left.

At two o'clock the next morning soldiers were back, firing their AK47 assault rifles point-blank into the crowd and setting afire the buses and other vehicles

Pro-government troops forcibly remove student protesters from Tiananmen Square in 1989. Such military actions proved that China was not ready for democracy . . . yet.

that the demonstrators had previously used to barricade the square. Some demonstrators fought back, but it was hopeless. The PLA kept shooting. "One hundred students linked arms and faced the tanks," noted Harrison Salisbury in his *Tiananmen Diary.* "Then another hundred linked arms and they were shot. It is too sad to write."[76] Within a few hours a thousand protestors had died. Then the troops fanned out into Beijing's streets, killing thousands more. In the corner of a Beijing hospital, bodies were stacked atop each other like cordwood.

Salisbury noted in *Tiananmen Diary:*

Whatever the number of students killed on Tiananmen it was only a fraction of the public mowed down. . . . [T]hese casualties were not inflicted in the center of town but in the outskirts, where the conduct of the PLA had touched off a genuine people's war. Tens and hundreds of thousands of ordinary citizens sprang from houses and flats to oppose armor with bare hands.[77]

The Goddess of Democracy was among the casualties. Before millions of television viewers, a tank hit the statue and reduced it to rubble almost instantly. However, the idea of democracy could not be destroyed so easily. Cao Xinyuan, who had overseen the original statue's production, wrote in *Children of the Dragon:*

I envision a day when a replica, as large as the original and more permanent stands in Tiananmen Square, with the names of those who died there written in gold on its base. It may well stand there after Chairman Mao's mausoleum has, in its turn, been pulled down.[78]

Later that day the army's newspaper, *Liberation Daily*, celebrated the PLA's great victory over a "counterrevolutionary insurrection."[79]

Man Against Tank

One of the most riveting images of the bravery of the pro-democracy demonstrators came as a row of tanks rumbled single file down Beijing's Changan Avenue. Remarkably, one worker stood in the middle of the street to block them. "Why are you here?" he shouted at the tank's crew. "You have done nothing but create misery. My city is in chaos because of you."[80] For a

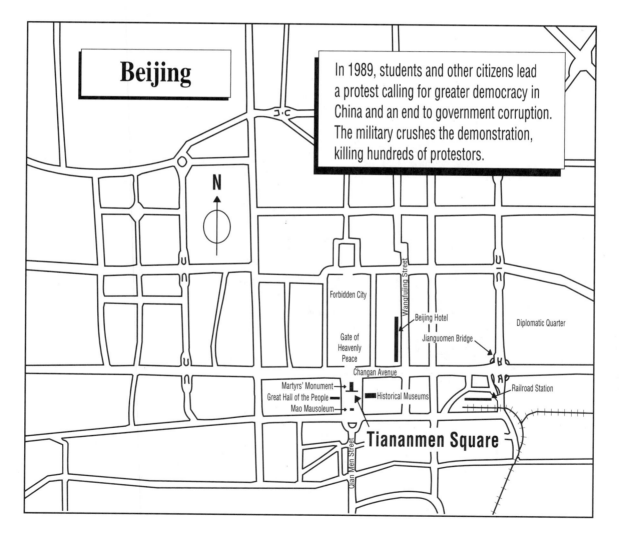

Beijing

In 1989, students and other citizens lead a protest calling for greater democracy in China and an end to government corruption. The military crushes the demonstration, killing hundreds of protestors.

N

Forbidden City

Wangfujing Street

Beijing Hotel

Diplomatic Quarter

Gate of Heavenly Peace

Jianguomen Bridge

Changan Avenue

Martyrs' Monument
Great Hall of the People
Mao Mausoleum

Historical Museums

Railroad Station

Tiananmen Square

Qian Men Street

while the worker stood his ground. The world watched in wonder, and in horror, at the spectacle. Would he be ground under the tank treads or, miraculously, could one brave and idealistic man halt this slaughter? The man climbed atop the turret of the lead tank, engaging in a dialogue with the soldiers, but then soldiers grabbed him and hustled him along. The tanks, and the repression, continued, but this unknown protestor had given the world a powerful symbol of the individual standing bravely against the brute force of totalitarian power.

China After Tiananmen

After the Tiananmen Square massacre, the world saw the People's Republic and Deng Xiaoping in a different light. Deng was no longer viewed as a force for reform, but rather as a tired old man who would stoop to any action to maintain his own dictatorship. The world began to see that although China had come a long way from the dark days of the Great Leap Forward and the Cultural Revolution, there were many issues that gave reason for concern.

The image of an unknown protestor halting a row of advancing tanks symbolizes to many the heroic bravery exhibited by those involved in the pro-democracy demonstration.

Despite Zhao Ziyang's ouster in 1989 and the triumph of the hard-liner faction around Deng Xiaoping, no one knows for certain which direction the party will take in the future. It was widely thought that unpopular premier Li Peng, the leader most often blamed for Tiananmen Square, would not be reelected to a second term, but despite an unusually large 11 percent of National People's Congress votes cast against him, he was reelected in March 1993.

Meanwhile, his rival Jiang Zemin quietly accumulated more and more power. Little is known personally about the colorless Jiang except that he can speak Russian, English, and Romanian. In March 1993 Jiang won election to the People's Republic presidency, becoming the only person besides Mao to simultaneously hold that post and the position of party leader. Clearly Jiang Zemin was the man to watch.

How long leaders like Li Peng and Jiang Zemin can maintain their grip on the world's most populous nation is not known. Increasingly, China's people thirst for change and freedom. The experience of the Soviet Union and its East European satellites suggests that communism is a system that can give way to democracy. Whether China will evolve toward political freedom peacefully and in a relatively short amount of time is not known. So many startling developments have already marked the short history of the People's Republic that it is no exaggeration to say that anything is possible.

Notes

Chapter 1: The East Is Red

1. Ross Terrill, *Mao: A Biography.* New York: Harper & Row, 1980, p. 55.
2. Quoted in Li Zhisui, with Anne F. Thurston, *The Private Life of Chairman Mao.* New York: Random House, 1994, p. 116.
3. Quoted in Dick Wilson, ed., *Mao Tse-Tung in the Scales of History.* London: Cambridge University Press, 1977, p. 40
4. John Byron and Robert Pack, *The Claws of the Dragon: Kang Sheng: The Evil Genius Behind Mao—and His Legacy of Terror in People's China.* New York: Simon & Schuster, 1992, p. 63.
5. Quoted in Byron and Pack, *The Claws of the Dragon*, p. 65.
6. Quoted in *Merriam Webster.'s Dictionary of Quotations.* Infopedia CD-ROM, Futurevision Multimedia, 1994.
7. Terrill, *Mao*, p. 99.
8. Quoted in Byron and Pack, *The Claws of the Dragon*, p. 225.
9. Quoted in Uli Franz, *Deng Xiaoping.* Boston: Harcourt Brace Jovanovich, 1988, p. 152.
10. Quoted in Zhisui, *The Private Life of Chairman Mao*, p. 304.

Chapter 2: China's Divided Leadership

11. Zhisui, *The Private Life of Chairman Mao*, p. 297.
12. Quoted in Zhisui, *The Private Life of Chairman Mao*, p. 379.
13. Byron and Pack, *The Claws of the Dragon*, p. 189.
14. Byron and Pack, *The Claws of the Dragon*, p. 20.
15. Quoted in Ross Terrill, *The White-Boned Demon: A Biography of Madame Mao Zedong.* New York: Touchstone, 1992, p. 136.
16. Terrill, *The White-Boned Demon*, p. 153.
17. Quoted in Martin Ebon, *Lin Piao: The Life and Writings of China's New Ruler.* New York: Stein & Day, 1970, p. 27.
18. Ebon, *Lin Piao*, p. 40.
19. Quoted in Ching Hua Lee, *Deng Xiaoping: The Marxist Road to the Forbidden City.* Princeton: Kingston Press, 1985, p. 115.
20. Quoted in Terrill, *Mao*, p. 269.

Chapter 3: The Cultural Revolution Begins

21. Quoted in Han Suyin, *Wind in the Tower: Mao Tsetung and the Chinese Revolution 1949–1975.* Boston: Little, Brown, 1976, p. 266.
22. Quoted in Anne F. Thurston, *Enemies of the People.* New York: Knopf, 1987, p. 89.
23. *Merriam Webster's Dictionary of Quotations.* Infopedia CD-ROM, Futurevision Multimedia, 1994.
24. Byron and Pack, and *The Claws of the Dragon*, p. 286.
25. Byron and Pack, *The Claws of the Dragon*, p. 299.
26. Quoted in Stanley Karnow, *Mao and China: From Revolution to Revolution.* New York: Viking, 1972, p. 230.

27. Quoted in Byron and Pack, *The Claws of the Dragon*, p. 344.

28. Quoted in Karnow, *Mao and China*, p. 230.

29. Franz, *Deng Xiaoping*, p. 184.

30. Thurston, *Enemies of the People*, p. 152.

31. Paul Johnson, *Modern Times: The World from the Twenties to the Eighties*. New York: Harper Colophon Books, 1983, p. 553.

32. Quoted in Terrill, *The White-Boned Demon*, p. 249.

33. Quoted in Terrill, *The White-Boned Demon*, p. 250.

34. Quoted in Terrill, *The White-Boned Demon*, p. 256.

Chapter 4: Red Guards, Red Terror

35. Quoted in Committee of Concerned Asian Scholars, *China! Inside the People's Republic*. New York: Bantam Books, 1972, p. 78.

36. Asia Research Centre, *The Great Cultural Revolution in China*. Rutland, VT: Charles E. Tuttle, 1968, p. 447.

37. Quoted in Hong Yung Lee, *The Politics of the Chinese Cultural Revolution: A Case Study*. Berkeley: University of California Press, 1978, p. 86.

38. Adrian Hsia, *The Chinese Cultural Revolution*. New York: McGraw-Hill, 1972, p. 160.

39. Quoted in Nien Cheng, *Life and Death in Shanghai*. New York: Grove Press, 1986, p. 67.

40. Quoted in Feng Jicai, *Voices from the Whirlwind: An Oral History of the Chinese Cultural Revolution*, New York: Pantheon, 1991, p. 52.

41. Lee, *The Politics of the Chinese Cultural Revolution*, p. 91.

42. Quoted in Asia Research Centre, *The Great Cultural Revolution in China*, p. 448.

Chapter 5: The Tide Turns

43. Terrill, *Mao*, p. 326.

44. Lee, *The Politics of the Chinese Cultural Revolution*, p. 249.

45. Quoted in Terrill, *Mao*, p. 327.

46. Quoted in Karnow, *Mao and China*, p. 441.

47. Quoted in Terrill, *Mao*, p. 329.

48. Quoted in Terrill, *Mao*, p. 329.

49. Zhisui, *The Private Life of Chairman Mao*, p. 514.

50. Quoted in Jicai, *Voices from the Whirlwind*, p. 95.

51. Quoted in Jicai, *Voices from the Whirlwind*, p. 94.

52. Zhisui, *The Private Life of Chairman Mao*, p. 513.

53. Quoted in Craig Dietrich, *People's China: A Brief History*. New York: Oxford University Press, 1986, p. 212.

Chapter 6: The Death of Lin Biao

54. Terrill, *The White-Boned Demon*, p. 304.

55. Quoted in Dietrich, *People's China*, p. 210.

56. Quoted in Yao Ming-Le, *The Conspiracy and Murder of Mao's Heir*. London: Collins, 1983, p. 68.

57. Quoted in Zhisui, *The Private Life of Chairman Mao*, p. 534.

58. Quoted in Byron and Pack, *The Claws of the Dragon*, p. 388.

59. Karnow, *Mao and China*, p. 467.

60. Quoted in Karnow, *Mao and China*, p. 346.

61. Quoted in Ming-Le, *The Conspiracy and Murder of Mao's Heir*, p. 127.

62. Quoted in Ming-Le, *The Conspiracy and Murder of Mao's Heir*, p. 66.

63. Quoted in Zhisui, *The Private Life of Chairman Mao*, p. 537.

64. Quoted in Karnow, *Mao and China*, p. 349.

Chapter 7: China After the Cultural Revolution

65. Quoted in Terrill, *The White-Boned Demon*, p. 367.

66. Dietrich, *People's China*, p. 213.

67. Quoted in Franz, *Deng Xiaoping*, p. 252.

68. Zhisui, *The Private Life of Chairman Mao*, p. 8.

69. Byron and Pack, *The Claws of the Dragon*, p. 414.

70. Quoted in Terrill, *The White-Boned Demon*, p. 372.

71. Quoted in Franz, *Deng Xiaoping*, p. 256.

72. Richard Evans, *Deng Xiaoping and the Making of Modern China*. New York: Viking, 1993, p. 226.

73. Quoted in Franz, *Deng Xiaoping*, p. 261.

74. Quoted in Human Rights in China, *Children of the Dragon: The Story of Tiananmen Square*. New York: Collier Books, 1990, p. 12.

75. Quoted in William R. Doerner, "Come Out! Come Out!: Mourning for a Fallen Leader Erupts into Defiant Demands for Political Change," *Time*, May 1, 1989, p. 44.

76. Harrison E. Salisbury, *Tiananmen Diary: Thirteen Days in June*. Boston: Little, Brown, 1989 p. 69.

77. Salisbury, *Tiananmen Diary*, p. 171.

78. Human Rights in China, *Children of the Dragon*, p. 179.

79. Quoted in Jesse Birnbaum and Howard G. Chua-Eoan, "Despair and Death in a Beijing Square," *Time*, June 12, 1989, p. 24.

80. Quoted in Strobe Talbott, "Defiance," *Time*, June 19, 1989, p. 10.

Glossary

big-character posters: Large propaganda posters of the Cultural Revolution; characters were often as large as a foot high.

cadre: A cell of indoctrinated leaders active in promoting the goals of a revolutionary party.

commissar: An official assigned to a military unit by the Chinese Communist Party to ensure loyalty to party principles and policies.

commune: A rural collective unit in which all land is held by the commune itself.

coup d'état: A French term for the seizure of power.

dynasty: A ruling royal family. China's last dynasty, the Qing, was overthrown in 1911.

five-year plans: Centralized economic plans first established in the Soviet Union by Joseph Stalin in 1928 and later used in the People's Republic of China; these plans emphasize rapid growth in heavy industry and agriculture during a five-year period.

Gang of Four: Radical faction of the Cultural Revolution, composed of Jiang Qing, Zhang Chunqiao, Yao Wenyuan, and Wang Hongwen.

general secretary: The highest office in the Chinese Communist Party (CCP).

Kuomintang: Also known as Guomintang or the KMT. The National People's Party; Chinese political party founded in 1912 by Song Jiaoren and refounded in 1919 by Sun Yat-sen and still in power in the Republic of China (ROC) on Taiwan (see **Republic of China**).

Manchukuo: Japanese puppet state that ruled Manchuria from 1932 to 1945.

Ming dynasty: The next-to-last Chinese dynasty. It ruled from 1368 to 1664.

People's Republic of China (PRC): The Communist government of China, proclaimed by Mao on October 1, 1949.

Politburo: Ruling council of the People's Republic of China (PRC); members were chosen by the Chinese Communist Party's Central Committee.

Republic of China (ROC): Founded by Sun Yat-Sen in 1911, the ROC under the leadership of Chiang Kai-shek battled Mao from the 1920s until its defeat in 1949. It remains in power to this day on the island of Taiwan.

secretariat: The office of the general secretary of the Chinese Communist Party (CCP).

Sichuanese: From the southern Chinese province of Sichuan.

socialism: Social organization based on government control of the production and distribution of goods and services.

struggle session: The process during the Cultural Revolution by which a person admitted his political errors. Often accompanied by harassment and violence.

totalitarianism: Political ideology calling for the domination of the individual person by the state and for all aspects of life to be controlled by the government.

warlord: A military commander who by force of arms holds both military and political control over a limited geographical area of a country.

yuan: The Chinese unit of currency, equivalent to the U.S. dollar. It is composed of ten jiao.

For Further Reading

Wendy Lubetkin, *Deng Xiaoping*. New York: Chelsea House, 1988. A readable, well-illustrated biography of Deng.

Albert Marrin, *Mao Tse-tung and His China*. New York: Viking Kestral, 1989. A highly useful biography of Mao that emphasizes his early career but contains a vividly written chapter on the chaos and brutality of the Cultural Revolution.

Valjean McLenighan, *People's Republic of China*. Chicago: Childrens Press, 1984. Contains just a brief chapter on the Cultural Revolution, but has much valuable information on what happened in the PRC both before and after the revolution, as well as material on life in China. Lavishly illustrated with many color photos.

Author's Note: The following film is valuable for gaining a deeper insight into the People's Republic and the Cultural Revolution:

To Live (1994), with Ge You, Gong Li, Niu Ben, Guo Tao, and Jiang Wu; directed by Zhang Zimou. The story of one Chinese family that survived the civil war, the Great Leap Forward, and the Cultural Revolution. A very well made film, but what is perhaps most surprising about *To Live* is the reaction of the Chinese government to it. Although *To Live* is far from being a scathing denunciation of Maoism or the Communist system, its director, Zhang Zimou, and its female star, Gong Li, were banned not only from filmmaking for two years following its release but also from speaking about the film. (Not rated.)

Works Consulted

Asia Research Centre, *The Great Cultural Revolution in China*. Rutland, VT: Charles E. Tuttle, 1968. A sourcebook of original documents on the Cultural Revolution. Contains a very detailed chronology of events from November 1965 to November 1966.

Jesse Birnbaum and Howard G. Chua-Eoan, "Despair and Death in a Beijing Square," *Time*, June 12, 1989. A vivid short account of the Tiananmen Square massacre.

A. Dane Bowen, "China's Problems Exorcising Mao," *Foreign Service Journal*, June 1991. A surprisingly lively short examination of how Deng Xiaoping dealt with the issue of Mao's reputation.

Fox Butterfield, *China: Alive in the Bitter Sea*. New York: Times Books, 1982. An overview of China written by the *New York Times* first Beijing bureau chief.

John Byron and Robert Pack, *The Claws of the Dragon: Kang Sheng: The Evil Genius Behind Mao—and His Legacy of Terror in People's China*. New York: Simon & Schuster, 1992. A truly excellent biography of one of Mao's worst henchmen and a startling look at how the People's Republic *really* operated.

Ching Hua Lee, *Deng Xiaoping: The Marxist Road to the Forbidden City*. Princeton: Kingston Press, 1985. A somewhat academic biography of Deng.

Committee of Concerned Asian Scholars, *China! Inside the People's Republic*. New York: Bantam Books, 1972. Contains a chapter on the Cultural Revolution, which in view of what we know today now seems unbelievably naive.

Craig Dietrich, *People's China: A Brief History*. New York: Oxford University Press, 1986. A very well organized general history of the PRC.

William R. Doerner, "Come Out! Come Out!: Mourning for a Fallen Leader Erupts into Defiant Demands for Political Change," *Time*, May 1, 1989. A review of the forces and events that led to the Tiananmen Square protest of 1989.

Martin Ebon, *Lin Piao: The Life and Writings of China's New Ruler*. New York: Stein & Day, 1970. This book features more of Lin's writings and speeches than information on his life.

Richard Evans, *Deng Xiaoping and the Making of Modern China*. New York: Viking, 1993. A good standard biography of Deng.

Feng Jicai, *Voices from the Whirlwind: An Oral History of the Chinese Cultural Revolution*. New York: Pantheon, 1991. The often tragic first-person stories of many individuals who lived through the Cultural Revolution.

Uli Franz, *Deng Xiaoping*. Boston: Harcourt Brace Jovanovich, 1988. Another good standard biography of Deng. Written before Tiananmen Square.

Marilyn Greene, "Challenging China; Ex-Prisoner: Million in Labor Camps," *USA Today*, July 27, 1992. News account of a former political prisoner in the PRC.

Han Suyin, *The Wind in the Tower: Mao Tsetung and the Chinese Revolution 1949–1975*. Boston: Little, Brown, 1976. A veteran observer of Mao's China offers her insights on his rule.

Hong Yung Lee, *The Politics of the Chinese Cultural Revolution: A Case Study*. Berkeley: University of California Press, 1978. A very technical and academic study of the inner workings of Red Guard organization.

Adrian Hsia, *The Chinese Cultural Revolution*. New York: McGraw-Hill, 1972. A study of the Cultural Revolution written from a non-Western perspective.

Human Rights in China, *Children of the Dragon: The Story of Tiananmen Square*. New York: Collier Books, 1990. A lavishly illustrated look at the Tiananmen Square protest and massacre, featuring many firsthand accounts of events.

Human Rights Watch World Report 1992, "Asia Watch: China and Tibet." *CNN Newsroom Global View CD-ROM*, Softkey, 1994. A very detailed and invaluable summary of human rights abuses in China since Tiananmen Square.

Paul Johnson, *Modern Times: The World from the Twenties to the Eighties*. New York: Harper Colophon Books, 1983. A brilliantly well written general history of the twentieth century with short sections on the PRC and the Cultural Revolution.

Stanley Karnow, *Mao and China: From Revolution to Revolution*. New York: Viking, 1972. More than just a biography of Mao, the book contains many fascinating individual stories from the Cultural Revolution.

Michael Y. M. Kau, *The Lin Piao Affair: Power Politics and Military Coup*. White Plains, NY: International Arts and Sciences Press, 1975. A standard study of the fall of Lin Biao.

Li Zhisui, with Anne F. Thurston, *The Private Life of Chairman Mao*. New York: Random House, 1994. Perhaps the most inside look we will ever have at the workings of Mao's inner circle. Very readable.

Liang Heng and Judith Shapiro, *After the Nightmare: Inside China Today*. New York: Collier Books, 1987. The story of a former Red Guard's return to the People's Republic.

———, *Son of the Revolution*. New York: Knopf, 1983. Memoirs of a survivor of the Cultural Revolution, whose involvement began as a twelve-year-old member of the Red Guards.

Nien Cheng, *Life and Death in Shanghai*. New York: Grove Press, 1986. The memoirs of a middle-class survivor of the Cultural Revolution. Told from the perspective of a Chinese woman who had spent many years in the West prior to 1949.

"Nixon's Final Words," *Time*, May 2, 1994. Nixon's final thoughts on Mao, Deng, and relations with China.

Harrison E. Salisbury, *Tiananmen Diary: Thirteen Days in June*. Boston: Little, Brown, 1989. A veteran reporter's notes on the massacre, written from inside China.

Strobe Talbott, "Defiance," *Time*, June 19, 1989. A look at the Tiananmen Square crackdown of June 1989.

Ross Terrill, *Mao: A Biography*. New York: Harper & Row, 1980. One of the standard biographies of Mao. Despite having been written before much new material was available, it still holds up well.

———, *The White-Boned Demon: A Biography of Madame Mao Zedong*. New York: Touchstone, 1992. An extremely readable biography of Jiang Qing, which reveals the web of intrigue that surrounded Mao and the Chinese leadership.

Anne F. Thurston, *Enemies of the People*. New York: Knopf, 1987. Personal stories of those who survived persecution during the Cultural Revolution.

Time, "Deng Xiaoping Leads a Far-Reaching, Audacious but Risky Second Revolution," January 6, 1986. An interesting profile of Deng, whom *Time* named as its Man of the Year. Written before the crackdowns on the pro-democracy movement.

Maslyn Williams, *The East Is Red: The View Inside China*. New York: William Morrow, 1967. A very sympathetic look at Maoism, written from the perspective of the 1960s.

Dick Wilson, ed., *Mao Tse-Tung in the Scales of History*. London: Cambridge University Press, 1977. A somewhat dry examination of Mao, divided into aspects of his leadership. Not a chronological biography.

Yao Ming-Le, *The Conspiracy and Murder of Mao's Heir*. London: Collins, 1983. The story of the Lin Biao affair told from Lin's side.

Zi-Ping Luo, *A Generation Lost: China Under the Cultural Revolution*. New York: Henry Holt, 1990. A personal memoir by a survivor of the Cultural Revolution.

Index

Picture Credits

Cover photo: Archive Photos
Archive Photos, 22 (bottom), 56, 73
Archive Photos/AFP, 50, 65
Archive Photos/AGIP, 75
AP/Wide World Photos, 12, 16, 21, 22 (top), 27, 30, 34, 36, 38, 41, 43, 45, 48, 53, 61, 66, 77, 82

National Archives, 20
New China Pictures/Eastfoto, 25, 31, 62, 70
Reuters/Bettmann, 80
Reuters/Paty Benic/Archive Photos, 79
UPI/Bettmann, 11

About the Author

David Pietrusza has written for numerous publications including *Modern Age*, the *Journal of Social and Political Studies*, *Academic Reviewer*, and the *New Oxford Review*. Several of his books, *The End of the Cold War*, *The Invasion of Normandy*, *The Battle of Waterloo*, and *The Mysterious Death of John F. Kennedy*, have been previously published by Lucent Books.

In addition Mr. Pietrusza has also written extensively on the subject of sports. He is the president of the Society for American Baseball Research (SABR) and managing editor of *Total Baseball*, the official encyclopedia of Major League Baseball. He has written four books on baseball (*Lights On!*, *Minor Miracles*, *Major Leagues*, and *Baseball's Canadian-American League*) and one on basketball (*The Phoenix Suns*). He is currently working on a major biography of baseball's first commissioner, Kenesaw Mountain Landis. In 1994 Pietrusza served as a consultant for the PBS Learning Link on-line system and produced the documentary "Local Heroes" for PBS affiliate WMHT.

He lives with his wife, Patricia, in Scotia, New York.